Confronting Chaos:
The Civility Crisis

NELSON R. GRIMMETT

DEDICATION

I dedicate this book to the youth of today, with the fervent hope that sanity and reason will prevail, love will unite, peace may abound, and Jesus Christ will be glorified. My generation (Gen X) broke this world. It is up to you to fix it. Blessed are the peacemakers, for they shall see God. I challenge you to love "colorblind".

CONTENTS

ACKNOWLEDGMENTS

I thank my dear friend, Cynthia Sosa, for being a light in a dark place, an inspiration and encourager, and a true Christian. I also want to thank Rev. Jeremy Travis, and all his awesome family, for their friendship, encouragement, and support.

INTRODUCTION

In contemporary America, there have been noticeable changes in the dynamics of civility, diverging significantly from previous norms. Historically, there was a general adherence to codes of conduct that emphasized respect, courtesy, and decorum in public discourse. However, the present era is characterized by a noticeable erosion of these traditional standards, creating an atmosphere marked by increased polarization, hostility, and a widespread lack of civility.

One significant change from previous generations is the widespread use of digital platforms and social media, which has fundamentally altered communication dynamics. While these technological advancements have enabled unprecedented connectivity and information dissemination, they have also provided a fertile ground for the spread of negativity, misinformation, and inflammatory rhetoric. The anonymity afforded by online interactions often emboldens individuals to engage in behaviors they might avoid in face-to-face encounters, leading to a coarser discourse and a magnification of divisive narratives.

Additionally, the fracturing of traditional social structures and the emergence of identity politics have played a role in the decline of civility in contemporary society. As individuals increasingly align themselves with narrower, more homogeneous groups based on ideology, ethnicity, or socioeconomic status, the sense of shared community and mutual respect diminishes. This fragmentation fosters an adversarial mentality, where differing viewpoints are seen not as opportunities for dialogue and understanding, but as opposing forces to be vehemently resisted.

While advocating for purported "tolerance," the intolerance of certain special interest groups has directly contributed to heightened incivility in the United States. For example, there have been instances where efforts to categorize the Bible as hate speech have surfaced in the political sphere, particularly within debates surrounding LGBTQ+ rights and other social issues. In 2019, a proposed bill in the California State Assembly gained attention for its intention to classify specific passages of the Bible as discriminatory and potentially subject to legal restrictions. Targeting verses addressing homosexuality, proponents of the bill argued that such passages promoted hate speech and advocated for their censorship (California AB2542 | 2019-2020 | Regular Session, n.d.). However, the proposal encountered significant opposition, with critics raising concerns about free speech and religious freedom. Although the bill did not pass, its introduction sparked a broader discourse about the boundaries of expression and the role of religious texts in public dialogue. Certain liberal factions continue to demonstrate intolerance towards conservative Christian beliefs and principles.

Beyond legislative efforts, there have been instances of advocacy groups and political figures calling for the Bible to be categorized as hate speech, particularly in educational settings. These calls often arise from concerns about the potential impact of biblical teachings on marginalized communities. However, such attempts are met with resistance from religious organizations and civil liberties advocates, who argue that labeling the Bible as hate speech undermines fundamental principles of freedom of religion and expression. These debates underscore the complex intersection of religion, politics, and individual rights in contemporary society.

Cancel culture is a contemporary social phenomenon characterized by collective ostracism or withdrawal of support for individuals, often public figures, perceived to have engaged in offensive or objectionable behavior. Within the political sphere, progressive liberal groups have been linked to advocating for cancel culture, to silence conservative voices and content that deviates from their ideological stances. Critics contend that this approach can impede open dialogue, curtail freedom of speech, and foster an environment where dissenting viewpoints are suppressed.

While the underlying intention of cancel culture is alleged by some as an effort to promote inclusivity and social justice, the methods employed have sparked discussions regarding the balance between holding individuals accountable and potentially stifling diverse perspectives in public discourse. It is crucial to foster constructive dialogue to address societal issues without inadvertently hindering the expression of diverse thoughts and viewpoints.

In present-day America, there is a growing concern regarding the rise of hostility and intolerance towards divergent viewpoints. Those who do not fully endorse a particular perspective risk being branded as hateful or violators of human rights. The freedom to think independently, influenced by personal experiences, faith, and values, appears to be dwindling. Many express apprehensions that the trend of cancel culture is diminishing freedom in America, as individuals face increasing scrutiny for not adhering to a specific ideology. The notion that holding a differing opinion or perspective infringes upon another person's human rights is viewed by many as nonsensical. Striking a balance between promoting inclusivity and preserving the freedom to express diverse opinions poses a complex challenge in our current social and political landscape.

Over the past decade, America has observed numerous instances of hostility and acts of violence arising from various movements, including those opposed to conservative, Christian, and pro-life ideologies. These incidents have frequently manifested as protests escalating into violence, targeted harassment, and tragic shootings. For instance, the 2017 shooting at a congressional baseball practice serves as a poignant example of the ramifications of extreme anti-Trump sentiments, wherein a gunman specifically targeted Republican lawmakers (Five people shot, including Republican congressman, at baseball practice, 2020). This event underscored the depth of political polarization and the hazards linked to ideological extremism in present-day America.

Furthermore, there have been numerous incidents of conservative speakers being silenced or subjected to physical violence on college campuses, reflecting an anti-conservative sentiment prevalent among certain activist groups. These actions not only suppress free speech but also create an atmosphere of fear and intimidation for individuals expressing conservative perspectives. Additionally, assaults on pro-life advocates outside abortion clinics and online harassment campaigns against those voicing Christian beliefs highlight the contentious nature of discussions surrounding faith and reproductive rights. These occurrences expose profound divisions within society, where ideological disparities frequently escalate into confrontations and, at times, violence.

Additionally, discussions regarding parental choice in education have occasionally erupted into conflicts, with tensions escalating between proponents of school choice and those who oppose specific educational policies. These clashes underscore the larger debate surrounding the government's role in influencing education and parental rights. It is blatantly clear that the past decade has witnessed a succession of concerning incidents that illustrate the difficulties presented by ideological polarization and emphasize the necessity for constructive dialogue and comprehension to foster unity in American society. The world has gone mad, and people seem angrier and more intolerant than ever before.

Antisemitism, characterized by hostility and prejudice against Jewish people, manifests in various forms, including violence, vandalism, and hateful rhetoric. Recent incidents, such as the one at Lakewood Church, underscore the imperative to address and combat antisemitism wherever it emerges (Today, 2024). Interestingly, there have been more than 400 attacks against Christian churches in the United States over the past few years. Shockingly, over 50 of these attacks were reportedly linked to pro-abortion advocates expressing their intolerance toward pro-life values (Kumar, 2022). This raises a fundamental question: where is the rationality in these actions? Disagreements, such as those regarding abortion, should not justify the burning of homes, churches, or businesses, or the assault of individuals and their families. The escalation of differing viewpoints into violence, destruction, and tragically, even death, is a troubling trend that challenges the principles of civil discourse and peaceful coexistence.

Why are people so filled with anger? Furthermore, why do they believe that their frustrations justify acts of incivility, destruction or theft of property, assault and battery, or even loss of life? From where did the notion arise that I must align with your perspective on every matter for you to extend respect, courtesy, and civility toward me? Does not the enforcement of ideologies through coercion and intimidation encroach upon my liberties? Indeed, it does.

Antisemitism has indeed seen an increase in various parts of the world, including the United States. Recent incidents include the vandalism of Jewish synagogues and cemeteries, verbal harassment directed at Jewish individuals, and the proliferation of online hate speech targeting Jews. These acts of antisemitism often stem from deep-seated prejudices and historical biases against Jewish people.

One significant factor contributing to the surge in antisemitism is the dissemination of misinformation and conspiracy theories, particularly through social media platforms. People who can't even find Palestine on a map are taking to the streets in angry protests and acts of intimidation and violence against Jews and Jewish sympathizers. It almost feels like a rebirth of Nazi Germany! These narratives frequently vilify Jews and perpetuate harmful stereotypes, fostering hatred and intolerance. Additionally, tensions in the Middle East, particularly those between Israel and Palestine, can sometimes exacerbate antisemitic sentiments. Criticisms of Israeli government policies may spill over into antisemitic rhetoric, resulting in discrimination and violence against Jewish communities.

Have you ever considered the logistics behind prolonged protests? Do the individuals involved not have responsibilities such as work or education? How do they maintain their presence in public areas, consistently causing disruption and attracting attention for extended periods? They must be receiving assistance from multiple channels. This raises the question: who would be motivated to finance such displays of unrest? Who stands to gain the most from funding or otherwise sustaining acts of aggression, violence, and intimidation? What motives could prompt someone to desire a society that is fractured, filled with hostility, and lacking clarity?

Protest movements frequently rely on financial support from a range of sources to sustain their activities over extended periods. This support can originate from individual donations, funding from organizations, crowdfunding campaigns, volunteer assistance, and grants or sponsorships. While some protesters may balance their participation with employment or educational commitments, others prioritize engaging in protests as a form of activism.

The financial assistance received is typically allocated towards covering various expenses associated with the protests. These may include transportation costs, meals, accommodation, legal fees, bail funds, and other protest-related expenditures. Sustaining a prolonged protest demands significant financial resources, and protesters often depend on a combination of these funding sources to continue their efforts over time. Who's pushing for America to be divided, and what's their motivation behind it? If you can answer those questions, you'll understand the root of this civility crisis.

The consequences of this decline in civility reach far and wide, with profound effects. It's more than just disagreements; the normalization of rudeness has led to a climate of distrust, hostility, and societal breakdown. Political discussions are now marked by constant arguing and stubbornness, making it hard to have meaningful conversations or find common ground. And it's not just in politics; this culture of rudeness has seeped into our everyday interactions, damaging relationships and making social tensions worse. What's most worrying is the impact on people's well-being. Studies show that exposure to rudeness is linked to higher levels of stress, anxiety, and poorer mental health.

When addressing the issues brought about by the civility crisis, it's crucial to understand the complexity of the problem and the importance of working together. We need to focus on building empathy, encouraging constructive conversations, and fostering a culture of respect to bring back the values of civility that are vital for a healthy society. Only by committing to these principles can we navigate the challenges of today's world and create a future defined by unity, empathy, and mutual respect.

I reject the idea that a person's value, competence, and ability to contribute to the world are based on their skin color or ethnicity. I don't have a racist bone in my body; in fact, most of my friends are people of color. Suggesting that I don't have to be inherently racist to have alleged privilege, engage in microaggressions, or oppress others is insulting on every level. We must stop the race-baiting and divisive politics. It's time to stop letting the media and special interest groups stoke frustration, anger, and hostility. We need to think for ourselves. The key to moving forward and healing as a society is to love without regard to color, let go of centuries-old injustices, and unite with purpose.

ix

CHAPTER 1

UNDERSTANDING THE CRISIS

Why Are People So Angry?

In 1992, riots erupted throughout Los Angeles after four police officers were acquitted of charges related to beating Rodney King. King made an impassioned plea for peace and harmony amid racial tensions when he said, *"Can't we all just get along?"* (Deb Kiner, dkiner@pennlive.com, 2019). That is an excellent question. Why can't we all just get along? Why are people so angry? Why are some people easily prone to acts of aggression, violence, and hostility?

Instead of engaging in introspection and genuine self-examination to respond to these inquiries with honesty and an open mind, many individuals opt for an easier route: attributing their hurt and systemic rage to external factors such as other people, circumstances, or socictal conditions. Some point fingers at concepts like "whiteness" and "white privilege," using them as a rationale for displaying incivility. Others attribute their pent-up anger to socioeconomic disparities, geographical constraints, or a multitude of other influences.

What happens when anger is allowed to fester? Unfortunately, it often leads to violence and aggression. In recent years, we've witnessed a troubling trend where Jewish people, Caucasians, and the elderly have become frequent targets of ethnic aggression. Mainstream media often attempts to justify these incidents and portray the victims as perpetrators. Even though slavery was abolished seven generations ago, almost 160 years ago, there seems to be a narrative that all Caucasians are inherently responsible for past injustices and should pay reparations. This viewpoint, propagated by lawmakers and special interest groups, is both absurd and damaging.

While it's crucial to acknowledge the complexities of societal issues such as systemic racism, some lawmakers have been criticized for defending criminal activity, such as looting, as a purportedly natural response to built-up rage stemming from systemic injustices. For instance, in certain instances, lawmakers have cited historical injustices and ongoing systemic racism as justification for criminal behavior, such as looting, during protests against police brutality. Additionally, there have been cases where politicians have made statements suggesting that looting and vandalism are understandable expressions of frustration and anger resulting from entrenched inequalities. These instances have sparked debate and controversy, with critics arguing that condoning criminal behavior undermines efforts to address systemic issues and perpetuates further harm to communities.

In times of turmoil, some exploit chaos and incivility to perpetrate acts of crime, all while cloaking themselves in the guise of righteous rage stemming from systemic racism. Just as Alfred Pennyworth astutely observed in "The Dark Knight," some individuals seem driven not by a desire for justice or reform, but by a destructive impulse to watch the world burn (*'Some People Just Want to Watch the World Burn' - the American Vision*, 2020). Within the context of protests against systemic injustices, these opportunists seize upon the unrest to engage in looting, burning, acts of violence, and the destruction of property. By hiding behind the narrative of societal anger and inequality, they not only betray the very communities they claim to represent but also inflict lasting harm, exacerbating the very injustices they purport to fight against.

In contemporary society, anger and frustration seem to permeate many facets of life, contributing to the erosion of civility and the rise of polarization. One key factor driving this anger is the deepening divide over fundamental beliefs and values. Whether it be matters of faith, ethical principles, or societal norms, individuals find themselves increasingly entrenched in opposing camps, each vehemently defending their perspectives. For example, debates over issues such as abortion, LGBTQ+ rights, and religious freedom often elicit intense emotional responses, with little room for compromise or understanding.

Moreover, the ever-expanding digital landscape has facilitated the rapid dissemination of information and the proliferation of echo chambers, where individuals are exposed only to viewpoints that align with their own. This phenomenon, known as confirmation bias, exacerbates divisions by reinforcing pre-existing beliefs and fostering a sense of righteous indignation towards those who hold differing opinions.

Defining Civility

Before delving into the complexities of the civility crisis, it is essential to establish a clear understanding of what civility entails. At its core, civility encompasses more than mere politeness or etiquette; it embodies a commitment to treating others with respect, empathy, and dignity, even in the face of disagreement. Civility entails active listening, open-mindedness, and a willingness to engage in constructive dialogue, recognizing that diverse perspectives enrich our understanding of the world.

However, civility does not require acquiescence or the suppression of dissenting views. Rather, it fosters an environment where disagreements can be navigated civilly, without resorting to personal attacks or hostility. In essence, civility is the foundation upon which meaningful discourse and democratic governance are built, serving as a bulwark against the corrosive effects of divisiveness and incivility.

Civility is a fundamental aspect of social interaction, encompassing a range of behaviors and attitudes that contribute to respectful and harmonious relationships within society. At its core, civility involves treating others with dignity, empathy, and kindness, regardless of differences in opinion, background, or identity. It entails engaging in discourse and disagreement with a spirit of openness and tolerance, fostering an environment where diverse perspectives can coexist and flourish.

Central to the concept of civility is the recognition of the inherent worth and humanity of every individual. It entails refraining from demeaning or belittling others, and instead, seeking to understand and empathize with their experiences and viewpoints. Civility involves active listening, genuine dialogue, and a willingness to consider alternative perspectives, even in the face of disagreement.

Moreover, civility encompasses a commitment to constructive engagement and peaceful conflict resolution. It entails expressing grievances or dissent in a manner that is respectful and nonviolent, eschewing aggression, hostility, or intimidation. By upholding principles of civility, individuals contribute to the creation of a social climate characterized by mutual respect, cooperation, and the pursuit of common goals.

Ultimately, civility serves as the foundation for a healthy and functional society, fostering trust, cohesion, and collective well-being. It enables individuals to navigate differences and disagreements peacefully, promoting social harmony and fostering a sense of community and belonging. In a world marked by diversity and complexity, the practice of civility is essential for building bridges, bridging divides, and cultivating a culture of mutual understanding and respect.

Historical Perspectives on Civility

Throughout history, civilizations have grappled with the challenge of maintaining civility amidst social, political, and cultural upheaval. From the ancient Greeks' emphasis on rhetoric and persuasion to the Enlightenment ideals of reason and tolerance, various societies have sought to cultivate norms of civility to foster social cohesion and progress.

In the United States, the founding fathers enshrined principles of civility and respect for differing viewpoints in the nation's founding documents, recognizing the importance of civil discourse in a pluralistic society. However, the historical trajectory of civility in America has been marked by periods of both progress and regression, from the civil rights movement of the 1960s to the partisan rancor of recent years.

Throughout American history, the concept of civility has evolved alongside societal norms, cultural shifts, and political developments. From the nation's founding to the present day, notions of civility have played a crucial role in shaping public discourse, interpersonal relations, and the functioning of democratic institutions.

In the early years of the republic, civility was often equated with the virtues of politeness, decorum, and deference to authority. Drawing on European traditions of etiquette and refinement, colonial elites sought to cultivate a sense of refinement and gentility in public life. However, this idea of civility was often reserved for the upper classes, while marginalized groups such as enslaved people, Native Americans, and women were excluded from the social contract and denied full citizenship rights (Miller, 2001).

As the nation expanded westward and underwent periods of profound social upheaval, the meaning of civility began to shift. During the Civil War era and Reconstruction, debates over the boundaries of civility were central to discussions about race, citizenship, and democracy. The struggle for civil rights and equality for African Americans challenged prevailing notions of civility, as activists like Frederick Douglass and Harriet Tubman demanded recognition of their humanity and dignity in the face of entrenched racism and discrimination (*The Civil Rights Movement | the Post War United States, 1945-1968 | U.S. History Primary Source Timeline | Classroom Materials at the Library of Congress | Library of Congress*, n.d.).

In the 20th century, the civil rights movement brought issues of civility to the forefront of national consciousness. Led by figures such as Martin Luther King Jr. and Rosa Parks, the movement sought to dismantle segregation and institutionalized racism, calling on Americans to live up to the ideals of equality and justice enshrined in the nation's founding documents (Onion, 2024). The quest for civil rights sparked fierce debates over the limits of civility, with proponents of segregation and white supremacy often invoking notions of "law and order" to justify violence and repression.

In contemporary America, debates over civility continue to shape political discourse and social dynamics. In an era marked by increasing polarization and divisiveness, calls for civility are often seen as a means of fostering dialogue and understanding across ideological divides. However, critics argue that appeals to civility can be used to silence dissent and maintain the status quo, particularly in the face of injustice and inequality. As the nation grapples with pressing challenges such as systemic racism, economic inequality, and political polarization, the meaning of civility remains a subject of ongoing debate and reflection.

Should we look toward past injustices as justification for hostile and lawless behavior in modern times? Martin Luther King Jr. didn't seem to think so. He said, *"Darkness cannot drive out darkness; only light can do that. Hate cannot drive out hate; only love can do that."* This quote from Martin Luther King Jr. emphasizes the transformative power of love and light in overcoming hatred and darkness (Philosiblog, 2013). It speaks to the importance of fostering a culture of civility and compassion in society, where understanding and empathy are prioritized over divisiveness and conflict. By promoting love and understanding, individuals can work towards building a more peaceful and harmonious world.

The Evolution of Discourse

Martin Luther King Jr. and Malcolm X, towering figures in the civil rights movement, diverged in their beliefs, tactics, and approaches toward achieving racial equality. King, rooted deeply in his Christian faith, advocated for nonviolent resistance and civil disobedience as the most potent tools for social change. His philosophy, grounded in love and moral persuasion, sought to appeal to the conscience of America, emphasizing the inherent dignity of all individuals regardless of race. In contrast, Malcolm X initially embraced a more militant stance, influenced by his affiliation with the Nation of Islam, advocating for self-defense and separatism. However, his pilgrimage to Mecca led to a transformation, prompting him to adopt a more inclusive approach toward racial justice.

King's tactics centered on peaceful protests, boycotts, and marches, aiming to challenge segregation and discrimination without resorting to violence. His strategy focused on building broad-based coalitions and leveraging moral authority to effect change within the existing political system. Conversely, Malcolm X, particularly during his tenure with the Nation of Islam, endorsed self-defense and armed resistance against racial oppression, though he later moderated his approach. Post-Mecca, he shifted toward advocating for political and economic empowerment within the black community, seeking to address systemic injustices from within (Mamiya, 2024).

Their differing approaches reflected broader philosophical disparities within the civil rights movement. King emphasized the necessity of working within the system, forging alliances with sympathetic whites and engaging in nonviolent direct action to enact legislative and social reforms. In contrast, Malcolm X initially viewed the system with skepticism, advocating for more radical forms of resistance, but later acknowledged the potential for political engagement and coalition-building. It should be understood that Malcom X and Martin Luther King Jr. held two very different views on how to combat systemic racism and work toward equality. Martin Luther King Jr. was a man of faith and a peacemaker while Malcom X advocated extreme views that often led to incivility and fractured relationships in society.

A radical concept Malcolm X espoused was black separatism, advocating for the establishment of separate institutions and communities exclusive to African Americans (BlackPast, 2019). He argued that such separation was necessary for black Americans to achieve autonomy and self-determination in the face of systemic oppression. Embracing the ideals of black nationalism, Malcolm X urged African Americans to reclaim their cultural identity and heritage, emphasizing the importance of black pride and self-respect as foundational to the struggle for racial equality.

Black nationalism is a political and social movement that advocates for the empowerment, self-determination, and solidarity of African Americans. It emphasizes the importance of black pride, identity, and cultural heritage, aiming to challenge systemic racism and promote the interests of the black community. Black nationalists seek to create autonomous institutions and communities where African Americans can exercise control over their own affairs and pursue social, economic, and political equality. In contrast, Marxism is a socio-political theory that focuses on class struggle and the need for a proletarian revolution to overthrow capitalism and establish a socialist society (Stephen, 2023). While both ideologies critique systemic oppression and advocate for social change, black nationalism prioritizes racial identity and empowerment within a specific racial group, whereas Marxism emphasizes class struggle and the collective liberation of the working class, transcending racial boundaries. Additionally, while black nationalism often emphasizes cultural and economic self-sufficiency within existing social structures, Marxism advocates for the complete overhaul of the capitalist system in favor of a classless society.

Ironically, some leaders within the Black Lives Matter (BLM) movement have expressed support for certain Marxist ideals and views, particularly in their critiques of systemic oppression and calls for radical social change (Kertscher, 2020). The movement's founders have openly identified as Marxists and have highlighted the importance of addressing economic inequalities alongside racial injustice. Additionally, the BLM movement has emphasized the need for collective action and solidarity in challenging structural racism and advocating for racial equality, echoing themes central to Marxist thought. However, it's essential to recognize that the BLM movement is diverse and decentralized, with various leaders and participants holding a range of ideological perspectives. While some individuals within the movement may align with Marxist principles, others may not, reflecting the multifaceted nature of the BLM movement and its commitment to addressing racial injustice through diverse tactics and strategies. Thus, what began as genuine efforts to combat systemic racism has transformed into deep-rooted ideals that want to undermine and replace the American capitalist system in favor of Marxism.

Patrisse Cullors, one of the co-founders of the Black Lives Matter (BLM) movement, has openly referred to herself and fellow co-founder Alicia Garza as "trained Marxists." In interviews, Cullors has discussed how she and Garza have extensively studied Marxist theory and ideologies, indicating that they incorporate this knowledge into the organizational framework of BLM (Steinbuch, 2020). This acknowledgment has sparked discussions about the ideological foundations of the BLM movement and prompted an examination of the influence of Marxist thought within its ranks.

It's important to note that not all members or supporters of BLM necessarily align themselves with Marxism. However, Cullors' statement highlights the diverse range of perspectives and ideologies that contribute to the movement's advocacy for racial justice and systemic change. Some observers have noted parallels between BLM's approach and the activism of Malcom X, focusing on more radical strategies for social reform, as opposed to the nonviolent tactics advocated by Martin Luther King Jr. for achieving true equality.

In a notable instance, Maxine Waters, a prominent political figure, stirred controversy by publicly advocating for aggression, confrontation, and intimidation towards then-President Donald Trump and his supporters. In a speech delivered at a rally, Waters urged supporters to "push back" against Trump administration officials and to confront them wherever they were seen in public spaces (Davis, 2018). Her remarks were widely interpreted as a call for heightened confrontation and incivility towards political adversaries. Critics argued that such rhetoric could contribute to a toxic political climate and potentially incite violence. While Waters defended her statements as a form of peaceful protest and resistance, the incident sparked intense debate about the boundaries of political discourse and the responsibility of public figures to promote civility and unity. Indeed, it is hard to see such rhetoric as calls for peaceful protests when Waters made statements like, *"They're Not Welcome Anymore, Anywhere"* (*Yahoo Is Part of the Yahoo Family of Brands*, 2018). Rather, her words obviously call for incivility, aggression, and intolerance of others.

It appears that hostility, aggression, violence, fear-mongering, and incivility have become normalized in modern society. The evolution of discourse in America reflects broader societal shifts in communication norms, technology, and cultural values. In the early days of the republic, political debates were conducted through pamphlets, newspapers, and public forums, where reasoned arguments and rhetorical skills held sway. However, the advent of radio, television, and, more recently, social media has transformed the nature of discourse, amplifying voices and accelerating the pace of communication.

Recently, the city of College Park, Maryland hired Kayla Aliese Carter as their racial equity officer. Carter appears to wholeheartedly embrace Marxist views, as well as a rhetoric of incivility and intolerance. Carter works with activists who champion statements like, *"Let's burn it all down"* and *"My ideology can rise from the ashes"* (Grossman, 2024b). Statements like this showcase how Carter, and others who think like her, do not embrace civility and tolerance. Rather, they have an agenda that divides ethnic groups and communities.

The rise of cable news networks and online media outlets has led to the fragmentation of the information landscape, with individuals gravitating towards sources that reinforce their existing beliefs. This phenomenon, often referred to as the "echo chamber effect," fosters insularity and reinforces ideological divides, making it increasingly difficult to bridge the gap between opposing viewpoints (Rebecca.Chalif, 2022).

In this digital age, the instantaneous nature of communication has also fueled the proliferation of incivility and vitriol, as individuals can easily disseminate inflammatory rhetoric and engage in anonymous attacks without fear of repercussions. This democratization of discourse, while empowering in many respects, has also opened the floodgates to a torrent of uncivil behavior, undermining the foundations of civil society.

As we navigate the complexities of the civility crisis, it is imperative to recognize the interplay between historical precedents, cultural shifts, and technological advancements shaping the contours of contemporary discourse. Only by understanding these dynamics can we begin to address the root causes of incivility and chart a path towards a more civil and respectful public sphere.

CHAPTER 2

THE RISE OF INCIVILITY

In the contemporary landscape, media outlets wield significant influence in shaping public discourse and perceptions. The proliferation of 24-hour news cycles, cable news networks, and online media platforms has heightened competition for viewership, leading to a focus on sensationalism and conflict-driven narratives. Sensationalist reporting prioritizes attention-grabbing headlines and provocative content over nuanced analysis and factual accuracy, often amplifying discord and exacerbating societal divisions.

Moreover, the advent of opinion-based journalism has blurred the lines between news and commentary, fostering an environment where subjective viewpoints and ideological biases often masquerade as objective reporting. This phenomenon, sometimes referred to as the "echo chamber effect," reinforces existing beliefs and entrenches partisan divides, as individuals gravitate towards media sources that confirm their preconceived notions while dismissing opposing viewpoints.

The pursuit of ratings and advertising revenue incentivizes media outlets to prioritize controversy and spectacle over substance and civility. As a result, issues that lend themselves to sensationalized coverage, such as political scandals, cultural controversies, and acts of violence, receive disproportionate attention, fueling public outrage and exacerbating societal discord.

The role of media influence and sensationalism in the rise of incivility in America cannot be overstated. In an era where news cycles move at breakneck speed and competition for viewership is fierce, many media outlets have resorted to sensationalizing stories to capture attention. This trend has led to a focus on divisive and controversial topics, often at the expense of balanced and nuanced reporting. As a result, news coverage tends to highlight conflict and confrontation, amplifying tensions and polarizing public discourse.

Moreover, the rise of social media has further exacerbated this issue. Platforms like Twitter and Facebook provide a breeding ground for sensationalism, where provocative headlines and inflammatory rhetoric spread rapidly, often without regard for accuracy or context (MacGillis, 2023). This has created echo chambers where individuals are exposed only to information that aligns with their preconceived beliefs, reinforcing ideological divides and undermining civil dialogue.

In this hyper-partisan media landscape, politicians and public figures also play a role in perpetuating incivility. Some individuals exploit sensationalized narratives to advance their own agendas, using fearmongering and divisive rhetoric to mobilize their base or demonize their opponents. This "us versus them" mentality fosters hostility and animosity, making it increasingly difficult to find common ground and work towards constructive solutions to pressing issues (Philosophy & Philosophy, 2023).

To what degree do politicians and the mainstream media influence the crisis of civility? I would argue that both play significant roles in exacerbating the situation. In other words, they hold the spoon and stir the pot. What they do appears intentional, strategic, and malevolent. Why would anyone want to spur chaos, incivility, confusion, and destruction in society? It's almost as though they want to see America collapse, fail, and become assimilated into a new world order.

In some of my earlier writings, I coined the term "the three D's" to describe how politicians operate: Deny, Denounce, and Defer. They often deny any wrongdoing, even when caught red-handed. They swiftly denounce anyone who questions or challenges their actions. Finally, they frequently defer blame onto others, seeking to conceal their ongoing involvement in the murky realms of corrupt politics. It doesn't matter whether you vote Republican or Democrat. They are all in bed together, working for their self-interests, and gradually making America less prosperous, less safe, and less civil.

For example, the United Nations (UN) secretary-general youth climate advisor recently called for Caucasians to be stripped of power across the globe (Grossman, 2024c). The blanket labeling of all white individuals as "the problem" is a gross oversimplification and a harmful generalization. Such assertions fail to acknowledge the vast diversity among white people and ignore the complexities of social issues. No one person or entity has the authority to make such sweeping and unsubstantiated claims. It's essential to recognize and address systemic inequalities and injustices without resorting to divisive language or assigning blame to entire racial groups.

Another example of politically motivated incivility can be seen in the recent movie entitled "American Society of Magical Negroes". The movie has a line in it that says white people are the world's most dangerous animals (Parks, 2024). That kind of racial rhetoric feeds division, hostility, and fear. What is the point of labeling all white people as the "most dangerous animal in the world"?

Democratic Party strategist James Carville appeared on national television on Wednesday March 20, 2024. He and Anderson Cooper talked blatantly about how Joe Biden should permit mob hits against Donald Trump and his supporters (A. Hall, 2024). How is this ethical, moral, and civil? It is a call for continued aggression and division. Such media pundits should be removed from network television!

Recently, there has been a call by activists in Boston for "white churches" to contribute $15 billion in reparations to the black community (Wehner, 2024). However, it's essential to recognize that the church is a universal entity, embracing individuals of all races, cultures, and backgrounds. The Apostle Paul emphasized this unity in Ephesians 2:16 and Ephesians 4:4, highlighting the concept of "one body" and one God. Moreover, Paul's teachings in Acts 17:26

underscore the truth that all humanity shares a common origin and essence, irrespective of ethnic distinctions. In essence, we all share the same humanity; our blood runs red.

Dividing communities along ethnic lines, particularly within religious contexts, is deeply concerning. Such actions breed animosity and undermine the fundamental unity of humanity. It's imperative to reject any ideology or rhetoric that fosters hatred or victimization based on ethnicity. Individuals should not be labeled as victims or victors based on their race. Any narrative promoting such division only serves to propagate falsehoods, sow discord, and foster confusion. Let us stand against such divisive ideologies and instead embrace the unity and love that transcends all cultural and racial boundaries.

Addressing the root causes of incivility in America requires a multifaceted approach. Media organizations must prioritize accuracy, fairness, and ethical reporting, resisting the temptation to prioritize clicks and views over journalistic integrity. Likewise, individuals must be vigilant consumers of media, critically evaluating sources and seeking out diverse perspectives to counteract the effects of echo chambers. Ultimately, fostering a culture of civility and respect will require collective effort from media professionals, politicians, and citizens alike, but it is essential for preserving the health of our democracy.

Polarization in Politics and Society

In recent years, political polarization has reached unprecedented levels, with deepening ideological divides permeating every aspect of public life. Partisan gridlock and ideological rigidity have stymied efforts at bipartisan cooperation, leading to a breakdown in civility and compromise within legislative bodies and political discourse more broadly.

The rise of identity politics and the politicization of social issues have further exacerbated divisions, as individuals increasingly align themselves with narrow, homogeneous groups based on race, ethnicity, religion, or socioeconomic status (*Identity Politics (Stanford*

Encyclopedia of Philosophy), 2020). This tribalistic mentality fosters an us-versus-them mentality, where differing perspectives are viewed not as opportunities for dialogue and understanding but as threats to be vehemently opposed.

Furthermore, the hyper-polarization of politics has given rise to the demonization of political opponents, as adversaries are portrayed as enemies to be defeated rather than fellow citizens with legitimate concerns and interests. This dehumanizing rhetoric degrades the quality of public discourse, making it increasingly difficult to find common ground or bridge partisan divides.

The rise of polarization in politics and society has been closely linked to the increase in incivility in America. In recent years, political divisions have become more entrenched, with individuals identifying strongly along partisan lines and viewing those with opposing viewpoints as adversaries rather than fellow citizens. This polarization has permeated all levels of society, from the halls of government to everyday interactions between friends and family members.

One of the key drivers of this polarization is the echo chamber effect, facilitated by social media and cable news networks. People are increasingly exposed to information that aligns with their existing beliefs, leading to the formation of ideological bubbles where dissenting opinions are dismissed or ignored. This echo chamber effect creates a fertile environment for the spread of incivility, as individuals are less likely to engage in civil discourse with those who hold different views.

Additionally, the rise of identity politics has contributed to polarization by emphasizing divisions based on race, gender, religion, and other social categories. Politicians and media outlets often exploit these divisions for political gain, stoking fear and resentment among different groups and deepening societal rifts. This "us versus them" mentality further fuels incivility, as individuals are encouraged to view those outside their own group as enemies to be defeated rather than fellow citizens to be engaged with respectfully (Trilling, 2022).

To address the rise of incivility fueled by polarization, it is essential to promote empathy, understanding, and open-mindedness. Encouraging civil discourse and constructive dialogue across ideological lines can help bridge divides and foster a sense of unity and common purpose. Additionally, efforts to combat misinformation and promote media literacy are crucial for breaking down echo chambers and fostering a more informed and engaged citizenry. Ultimately, overcoming polarization and reducing incivility will require concerted efforts from individuals, communities, and institutions across society.

Social Media and Online Discourse

The advent of social media platforms has revolutionized the way individuals communicate and interact, offering unprecedented opportunities for connectivity and information sharing. However, the unfiltered nature of online discourse has also created fertile ground for the spread of incivility, misinformation, and polarization.

Social media algorithms, designed to maximize user engagement, often prioritize sensationalist content and divisive narratives, amplifying outrage and exacerbating societal divisions. Echo chambers and filter bubbles further entrench individuals in ideological silos, insulating them from diverse perspectives and fostering confirmation bias (Menczer, 2021).

Moreover, the anonymity afforded by online interactions often emboldens individuals to engage in behaviors they might refrain from in face-to-face encounters, leading to a proliferation of trolling, harassment, and cyberbullying. This toxic environment undermines efforts at civil discourse and constructive dialogue, perpetuating a cycle of incivility and hostility.

As society grapples with the consequences of incivility in the digital age, it is imperative to address the role of media influence, political polarization, and online discourse in shaping public attitudes and behavior. Only by confronting these challenges can we hope to foster a more civil and respectful public sphere, where diverse perspectives are valued, and constructive dialogue thrives.

The advent of social media has transformed the landscape of public discourse in America, playing a significant role in the rise of incivility. Platforms like Twitter, Facebook, and Reddit have provided unprecedented opportunities for individuals to engage in public dialogue, but they have also facilitated the spread of vitriol and divisiveness. One of the key factors contributing to the rise of incivility on social media is the anonymity it affords users, enabling them to engage in behavior they might not exhibit in face-to-face interactions. This anonymity can embolden individuals to unleash their frustrations and grievances without fear of repercussions, leading to a toxic online environment characterized by harassment, bullying, and personal attacks.

Furthermore, social media algorithms often prioritize content that elicits strong emotional responses, such as outrage or indignation, to maximize user engagement. This has led to the proliferation of sensationalized and polarizing content, which can exacerbate existing societal divisions and fuel incivility. In addition, the echo chamber effect inherent in many social media platforms further compounds the problem by reinforcing users' existing beliefs and shielding them from opposing viewpoints. This creates a fertile breeding ground for extremism and intolerance, as individuals become increasingly isolated within their ideological bubbles and less willing to engage in civil discourse with those who hold different perspectives (Barberá, 2020).

Moreover, the instantaneous and global nature of social media allows misinformation and disinformation to spread rapidly, undermining the foundations of civil discourse and eroding trust in institutions and fellow citizens. Falsehoods and conspiracy theories can quickly gain traction online, sowing confusion and discord within society and further polarizing public opinion. In this environment, it becomes increasingly challenging to distinguish fact from fiction and engage in meaningful dialogue based on shared values and principles.

Addressing the role of social media in the rise of incivility requires a multifaceted approach that involves both technological and societal solutions. Platforms must take responsibility for moderating harmful content and promoting healthier online interactions, while users must exercise greater critical thinking and empathy in their online interactions. Additionally, efforts to promote media literacy and digital citizenship are crucial for equipping individuals with the skills they need to navigate the complexities of online discourse and engage in constructive dialogue across ideological divides. Ultimately, fostering a culture of civility and respect in the digital realm will require collective action from all stakeholders involved.

CHAPTER 3

NORMALIZING DESTRUCTIVE BEHAVIOR

Celebrity Culture and Its Impact

In contemporary society, celebrity culture exerts a profound influence on societal norms and values, often shaping perceptions of acceptable behavior and moral standards. Celebrities, as cultural icons and influencers, wield significant power in shaping public discourse and attitudes, particularly among younger generations.

However, the glorification of fame and fortune in celebrity culture can also serve to normalize destructive behavior, such as substance abuse, reckless behavior, and disregard for societal norms. The relentless pursuit of sensationalism and scandal in tabloid media perpetuates a cycle of voyeurism and sensationalism, where the private lives of public figures are scrutinized and commodified for public consumption.

Moreover, the idolization of celebrities who engage in controversial or morally dubious behavior can send the message that such conduct is not only acceptable but aspirational (Barneclo, 2021). This normalization of destructive behavior contributes to a broader cultural shift where sensationalism and spectacle take precedence over integrity and character.

Celebrity culture in America has long been intertwined with the normalization of destructive behavior and incivility. With the rise of tabloid media and reality television, celebrities have become larger-than-life figures whose every move is scrutinized and sensationalized for public consumption. This constant exposure often glamorizes reckless behavior, material excess, and conflict, sending a message to audiences that such behavior is not only acceptable but desirable (Juntiwasarakij, 2018).

Take, for instance, Jonathan Glazer's 2024 Oscars acceptance speech, which was criticized for containing antisemitic rhetoric (Lapin, 2024). This speech understandably angered millions of Jewish people worldwide. Like many others, I can't help but question why Jonathan, along with other celebrities, feel the need to inject political statements into such occasions instead of simply accepting their award. It's a common occurrence, and it seems intentional. Celebrities often use their popularity to spread politically motivated beliefs to a wide audience, even though these ideologies can often cause confusion, pain, division, and incivility.

One of the most concerning aspects of celebrity culture is the glorification of fame at any cost. Many individuals are willing to engage in outrageous or scandalous behavior in pursuit of notoriety, believing that fame and attention are the ultimate markers of success. This relentless pursuit of fame can lead to a culture of superficiality and narcissism, where individuals prioritize image and status over integrity and decency.

Moreover, celebrities often serve as role models for millions of fans, especially young people who may be impressionable and easily influenced. When celebrities engage in destructive behavior or exhibit incivility, it can have a ripple effect, normalizing such conduct and leading others to emulate it. This phenomenon is particularly pronounced in the age of social media, where celebrities have direct access to their fans and can exert a powerful influence over their attitudes and behaviors.

Additionally, the rise of celebrity influencers on platforms like Instagram and TikTok has further blurred the lines between celebrity culture and everyday life. These influencers often project a curated image of perfection and success, promoting materialism and consumerism while downplaying the realities of mental health struggles, personal challenges, and ethical responsibilities. This can create unrealistic expectations and foster a culture of comparison and envy, exacerbating feelings of inadequacy and dissatisfaction among audiences.

To tackle the influence of celebrity culture on the acceptance of harmful behavior and incivility, it's crucial to promote media literacy and critical thinking skills among the public. By urging individuals to question the messages they encounter in the media and to critically evaluate the values they endorse, we can start to challenge the negative norms promoted by celebrity culture. Moreover, it's important to hold celebrities accountable for their actions and encourage them to serve as positive role models. This shift can help foster a narrative centered around integrity, empathy, and respect. Ultimately, building a culture of civility and decency requires collaboration from all segments of society, including the entertainment industry and its audience.

Desensitization to Violence

In an era characterized by ubiquitous media exposure and the omnipresence of digital screens, individuals are increasingly desensitized to images of violence and suffering. The constant barrage of graphic content in news media, entertainment, and video games can numb individuals to the real-world consequences of violence, fostering a culture of apathy and indifference.

Furthermore, the normalization of violence in popular culture, including movies, television shows, and music, desensitizes audiences to its impact, portraying aggression and conflict as glamorous or exciting rather than tragic. This desensitization to violence can desensitize individuals to the suffering of others, eroding empathy and compassion, and fostering a callous disregard for human life (*Normalizing Sexual Violence Through Media Fuels Rape Culture – Saratoga Falcon*, 2021).

Various platforms and activities have contributed to the desensitization of America to violence and a diminishing sense of compassion towards others. One significant factor is the prevalence of violent imagery in popular media, including movies, television shows, video games, and online content. Exposure to graphic violence regularly can desensitize individuals to its impact, leading them to become numb or indifferent to the suffering of others (*Media Violence and Desensitization | Applied Social Psychology (ASP)*, 2023).

Moreover, the 24-hour news cycle and social media platforms often sensationalize violent events, inundating audiences with graphic images and sensationalized coverage. While the intention may be to inform the public, this constant barrage of violent imagery can have the unintended effect of normalizing violence and desensitizing viewers to its consequences. Over time, individuals may become desensitized to violence, viewing it as a routine aspect of daily life rather than a cause for alarm or concern.

If you weren't already aware of how mainstream media manipulates people, let me shed some light on it. Catchphrases like "fake news," "war on...," "radical or extremist," "crisis," "conspiracy theory," "misinformation," "degenerate," "thugs," "privileged," "deplorable," "Christian nationalists," and so on are woven into programming that reaches millions of viewers every day. When you're constantly told to be angry about something, eventually, you'll start feeling that way (Fleming, 2020). The media has become a protagonist in promoting anger and rage, both intentionally and strategically. They are skilled at creating a crisis where there was none and pitting people against each other without any rationale. The real question we should be asking ourselves is, why?

Social media enables the spread of anger, hate, and incivility as well. The anonymity and detachment afforded by online platforms can foster a culture of callousness and indifference towards others. Behind the anonymity of a screen, individuals may feel emboldened to engage in cyberbullying, harassment, or trolling behavior without considering the real-world impact on their targets. This lack of empathy and compassion towards others can erode the social fabric and contribute to a culture of division and hostility.

Furthermore, societal factors such as social inequality, systemic injustice, and political polarization can also contribute to a lack of compassion towards others. When individuals feel marginalized or disenfranchised, they may be less inclined to extend empathy towards those perceived as different from themselves. Similarly, political polarization can lead to the dehumanization of opponents, making it easier to justify acts of violence or cruelty toward those with opposing viewpoints.

To counteract the desensitization to violence and lack of compassion in American society, it is crucial to promote empathy, kindness, and understanding in all aspects of life. This includes fostering a media environment that prioritizes responsible and ethical reporting, promoting positive role models and narratives that emphasize empathy and compassion, and addressing systemic issues such as social inequality and injustice. By fostering a culture of empathy and compassion, we can work towards building a more caring and inclusive society where violence is not tolerated, and all individuals are treated with dignity and respect.

Reverse Racism and the Propagation of White Privilege

In recent years, discussions surrounding race and privilege have become increasingly contentious, with accusations of "reverse racism" and the propagation of "white privilege" dominating public discourse. While these concepts are intended to highlight systemic inequities and promote social justice, they can also fuel resentment and division among different racial and ethnic groups (Quarles, 2024).

The notion of "reverse racism" suggests that individuals from historically marginalized backgrounds can also exhibit prejudice and discrimination towards those in positions of privilege. I concur with this concept, having experienced instances of reverse racism throughout my career.

For instance, there was a situation where I applied for and was offered a promotion within an organization. However, my supervisor at the time, who happened to be a black male, informed me privately that I couldn't have the position. He explained that some of the other employees in the department, all of whom were black, expressed discomfort about working alongside a white man. This incident occurred in 2009, and it is indeed a factual occurrence.

In short, despite having been offered and accepted the promotion, I ultimately did not receive it due to the objections raised by certain colleagues. I did not get that job because I am a white male. I filed a grievance, but it was dismissed by the Equal Opportunity Office (EEO) because there is a prevalent mindset that racism only works in one direction. The erroneous belief is that white people are inherently racist and can never be victims of racism. That's a lie, my friends. While discrimination against any group is unacceptable, framing racism solely within the context of power dynamics can oversimplify the complexities of racial interactions and perpetuate a narrative of victimization.

Similarly, the notion of "white privilege" has sparked debate and controversy, with some arguing that it unfairly demonizes individuals based on their race while ignoring other forms of privilege and disadvantage (Malik, 2020). While acknowledging the existence of systemic inequities is crucial for promoting social justice, the vilification of individuals based on their race can exacerbate tensions and hinder efforts at reconciliation and understanding.

The promotion of critical race theory (CRT) and the assertions of white privilege and the "white gaze" have sparked intense debate and controversy in America, with critics arguing that these concepts contribute to increased incivility and societal division (Walsh, 2020). Proponents of CRT argue that it provides a valuable framework for understanding the pervasive influence of race and racism in American society, shedding light on systemic injustices and inequities that have historically marginalized people of color.

However, critics contend that CRT promotes a divisive and antagonistic view of race relations, framing all social interactions through the lens of power dynamics and perpetuating a narrative of victimhood and oppression. By emphasizing the role of white privilege and the "white gaze," CRT can create an us-versus-them mentality that pits racial groups against each other, fostering resentment and animosity instead of fostering understanding and cooperation.

Moreover, the focus on white privilege and the "white gaze" undermines efforts to foster unity and reconciliation in a diverse society. By assigning blame and responsibility based on race, CRT can alienate individuals and communities, reinforcing stereotypes and prejudices instead of challenging them. This can further entrench racial divisions and hinder efforts to build bridges and find common ground across racial lines.

Furthermore, the promotion of CRT in educational institutions and public discourse has led to backlash and controversy, with some arguing that it stifles free speech and intellectual diversity. Critics of CRT have raised concerns about its potential to indoctrinate students with a particular ideological viewpoint, discouraging critical thinking and open dialogue on complex issues related to race and identity.

Consequences of Normalization of Violence

The normalization of destructive behavior, whether through celebrity culture, desensitization to violence, or discussions surrounding race and privilege, has profound consequences for society as a whole. By blurring the lines between right and wrong and normalizing aggression and conflict, these cultural forces erode the moral fabric of society and undermine efforts at fostering empathy, compassion, and mutual respect.

Moreover, the normalization of violence perpetuates a cycle of harm and suffering, with profound implications for individuals and communities affected by its consequences. From the perpetuation of cycles of poverty and violence to the erosion of trust and social cohesion, the normalization of destructive behavior exacts a heavy toll on society, perpetuating a vicious cycle of conflict and division.

As society grapples with the normalization of destructive behavior, it is imperative to confront these cultural forces head-on and foster a culture of empathy, compassion, and mutual respect.

Only by challenging prevailing norms and values can we hope to build a more just, compassionate, and inclusive society for future generations.

The normalization of violence, aggression, hostility, and incivility in America has far-reaching consequences that permeate every aspect of society. Firstly, it erodes the foundations of civil discourse and democratic governance, as productive dialogue becomes increasingly difficult in an environment characterized by hostility and aggression (Sun et al., 2021). When individuals resort to personal attacks and inflammatory rhetoric rather than engaging in reasoned debate, it undermines the principles of mutual respect and cooperation essential for a functioning democracy.

Moreover, the normalization of violence and aggression can have a profound impact on mental and emotional well-being, both for individuals directly affected by acts of violence and for society as a whole (Rivara et al., 2019). Exposure to violent imagery and hostile interactions can desensitize individuals to the suffering of others and contribute to a culture of callousness and indifference. This can lead to increased rates of anxiety, depression, and trauma, as individuals struggle to cope with the pervasive sense of insecurity and fear.

Furthermore, the normalization of incivility and hostility can have dire consequences for social cohesion and community resilience. When trust and empathy are eroded by a culture of aggression and hostility, it becomes increasingly difficult to foster meaningful connections and build strong communities. This can lead to social isolation, alienation, and a breakdown of social bonds, exacerbating feelings of loneliness and disconnection among individuals.

Additionally, the normalization of violence and aggression perpetuates cycles of harm and perpetuates inequalities, particularly for marginalized and vulnerable populations. When violence and aggression are accepted as normal or justified, it can lead to the perpetuation of systemic injustices and the reinforcement of power imbalances. This further marginalizes already marginalized groups and undermines efforts to promote equality, justice, and human rights for all.

The normalization of violence, aggression, hostility, and incivility in America poses serious threats to the fabric of society and the well-being of individuals. By recognizing the harmful consequences of these behaviors and working collectively to promote empathy, understanding, and respect, we can strive towards building a more peaceful, equitable, and compassionate society for future generations.

Recently, an NYPD officer, Jonathan Diller, was shot in the stomach by a violent repeat offender named Guy Rivera during a routine traffic stop. Diller died. Many of us see situations like this resulting from the efforts of liberals who are working to defund the police. SBA President Vincent Vallelong said that the extreme left has been blinded by their hatred and twisted ideologies that they are intentionally making America less safe (Ruiz, 2024). In fact, according to Vallelong, the "defund police" advocates would rather see cities burn and countless lives lost than admit that their legislative policies are not working. According to Vallelong, liberal prosecutors who are willing to let violent criminals off the hook are contributors to the destruction of civilized society (Ruiz, 2024).

CHAPTER 4

ROOT CAUSES OF THE CIVILITY CRISIS

Lack of Empathy and Understanding

One of the foundational pillars of civil society is empathy — the ability to understand and share the feelings of others. However, amid the civility crisis, empathy appears to be in short supply. The breakdown of interpersonal connections, fueled by the rapid pace of modern life and the prevalence of digital communication, has contributed to a pervasive sense of disconnection and alienation.

Moreover, the echo chambers created by social media algorithms and the rise of partisan news sources have reinforced existing biases and insulated individuals from diverse perspectives. This insularity makes it increasingly difficult to empathize with those who hold different beliefs or life experiences, fostering an "us versus them" mentality that undermines efforts at constructive dialogue and mutual understanding.

The lack of empathy and understanding serves as a fundamental root cause of the civility crisis in America. Empathy, the ability to understand and share the feelings of others, is essential for fostering meaningful connections and promoting mutual respect in society. However, in an increasingly polarized and divided society, empathy has become a scarce commodity, replaced by suspicion, distrust, and animosity towards those perceived as different from ourselves (Hall & Leary, 2024).

One of the main drivers of this lack of empathy is the growing social and political polarization in America. When individuals retreat into ideological echo chambers and surround themselves only with like-minded individuals, they become less

29

exposed to diverse perspectives and experiences. This can lead to a lack of understanding and empathy towards those with different backgrounds or viewpoints, as individuals are less likely to engage in meaningful dialogue or seek common ground with those they perceive as adversaries.

Moreover, the rise of social media and online communication has further exacerbated this lack of empathy by facilitating the spread of misinformation, echo chambers, and cyberbullying. Behind the anonymity of a screen, individuals may feel emboldened to engage in hostile or aggressive behavior towards others, without considering the real-world impact of their actions. This can lead to a culture of callousness and indifference, where empathy and compassion are seen as weaknesses rather than strengths.

Additionally, systemic factors such as social inequality, economic insecurity, and racial injustice can also contribute to a lack of empathy and understanding in society. When individuals feel marginalized or disenfranchised, they may be less inclined to extend empathy toward others, focusing instead on their struggles and survival. This can further deepen divisions and perpetuate cycles of harm and injustice, making it increasingly difficult to foster a culture of civility and cooperation.

To address the civility crisis in America, it is essential to promote empathy and understanding as foundational values in society. This requires fostering diverse and inclusive spaces where individuals from different backgrounds can come together to listen, learn, and empathize with one another. Additionally, education and media literacy initiatives can help equip individuals with the skills they need to critically evaluate information, engage in civil discourse, and challenge their own biases and assumptions. By prioritizing empathy and understanding, we can work towards building a more compassionate, inclusive, and resilient society for all.

Tribalism and Identity Politics

In recent years, identity politics has emerged as a dominant force in shaping public discourse, with individuals increasingly defining themselves and others based on immutable characteristics such as race, gender, religion, or sexual orientation. While identity politics can serve as a powerful tool for advocating for marginalized communities and promoting social justice, it can also foster tribalism and division.

The tendency to prioritize group identity over individual autonomy can lead to the demonization of perceived outsiders and the exclusion of dissenting voices within one's community. This tribalistic mentality exacerbates societal divisions and impedes efforts at building bridges across ideological and cultural divides (*Identity Politics (Stanford Encyclopedia of Philosophy)*, 2020b).

Moreover, the politicization of identity can create a zero-sum mentality, where gains for one group are perceived as losses for another. This competitive dynamic undermines efforts at coalition-building and compromises, fostering a climate of distrust and animosity that hinders progress on pressing social issues.

Tribalism and identity politics are significant root causes of the rise of incivility in America, fueling divisiveness and animosity between different groups within society. Tribalism refers to instinctive loyalty and identification with a particular group, often at the expense of cooperation and understanding with those outside of the group (Davidai & Ongis, 2019). In today's polarized political climate, individuals increasingly identify with their political party, ideological movement, or social identity, viewing those who disagree with them as enemies rather than fellow citizens.

Identity politics, on the other hand, involves the prioritization of political and social issues based on characteristics such as race, gender, sexuality, or religion. While identity politics can serve as a means of amplifying the voices of marginalized groups and addressing systemic injustices, it can also lead to the balkanization of society, where individuals view themselves primarily through the lens of their identity group and perceive others as adversaries based on their group affiliation (Reporter, 2021).

Both tribalism and identity politics contribute to the rise of incivility by fostering an us-versus-them mentality, where individuals are more focused on defeating their opponents than finding common ground or seeking compromise. This can lead to a toxic political environment characterized by demonization, dehumanization, and the vilification of those with opposing viewpoints. Instead of engaging in civil discourse and respectful debate, individuals may resort to personal attacks, character assassination, and hostile rhetoric to score political points or defend their group identity.

Furthermore, tribalism and identity politics can exacerbate social divisions and perpetuate cycles of mistrust and resentment between different groups within society. When individuals prioritize their group identity above all else, it can lead to the exclusion and marginalization of those who do not fit within the dominant narrative. This can further deepen societal rifts and hinder efforts to build bridges and foster understanding between different communities.

In order to address the rise of incivility fueled by tribalism and identity politics, it is essential to promote empathy, understanding, and respect for diverse perspectives. This requires fostering inclusive spaces where individuals from different backgrounds can come together to engage in meaningful dialogue and exchange ideas. Additionally, efforts to bridge divides and build social cohesion must involve addressing underlying inequalities and systemic injustices that contribute to feelings of alienation and resentment among marginalized groups. By prioritizing empathy and understanding, we can work towards creating a more inclusive, equitable, and harmonious society for all.

Economic and Social Disparities

Rooted in centuries of systemic inequality and injustice, economic and social disparities continue to exacerbate divisions within society. As wealth and opportunity become increasingly concentrated in the hands of a privileged few, marginalized communities are left behind, trapped in cycles of poverty and despair.

Economic insecurity breeds resentment and frustration, as individuals struggle to make ends meet and provide for their families. Moreover, the erosion of social safety nets and the dismantling of public services exacerbate feelings of alienation and disenfranchisement, fueling anger and resentment toward those perceived as benefiting from the status quo (Sherman et al., 2021).

The widening gap between the haves and the have-nots not only undermines social cohesion but also perpetuates a sense of injustice and inequality that fuels social unrest and unrest. As long as economic and social disparities persist, efforts at fostering civility and mutual respect will continue to be undermined by deep-seated grievances and inequalities.

Economic and social disparities serve as significant root causes of the rise of incivility in America, exacerbating divisions and fostering resentment among different segments of society. The widening gap between the wealthy elite and the working class has created a sense of economic insecurity and disillusionment among many Americans, fueling feelings of resentment and alienation towards those perceived as benefiting from a rigged system. This sense of economic injustice can lead to frustration and anger, which may manifest in acts of incivility towards perceived symbols of wealth and privilege (Lavizzo-Mourcy et al., 2021).

Furthermore, social disparities, including racial inequality, gender discrimination, and systemic injustice, contribute to feelings of marginalization and disenfranchisement among historically marginalized communities. When individuals feel excluded or disadvantaged due to their race, gender, or socioeconomic status, it can lead to feelings of resentment and anger towards those perceived as holding power and privilege. This can further deepen divisions and perpetuate cycles of mistrust and animosity between different groups within society.

Moreover, economic and social disparities can exacerbate social fragmentation and erode social cohesion, as individuals retreat into their own social and cultural enclaves in search of belonging and security. This can lead to the formation of echo chambers and ideological bubbles, where individuals are exposed only to perspectives that reinforce their existing beliefs and prejudices. This can further entrench divisions and hinder efforts to foster empathy, understanding, and cooperation between different groups within society.

Addressing the root causes of incivility fueled by economic and social disparities requires comprehensive efforts to address underlying inequalities and promote social justice and economic opportunity for all. This includes initiatives to reduce income inequality, ensure access to quality education and healthcare, and dismantle systemic barriers to advancement and inclusion. Additionally, efforts to foster empathy, understanding, and respect for diverse perspectives are crucial for bridging divides and building social cohesion in a diverse and rapidly changing society. By prioritizing equity and inclusion, we can work towards creating a more just, harmonious, and civically engaged society for all.

Instigators of Reverse Racism and Ethnic Tensions

In recent years, discussions surrounding race and ethnicity have become increasingly fraught, with accusations of "reverse racism" and the propagation of ethnic tensions dominating public discourse. While efforts to address systemic racism and promote equity and inclusion are crucial for fostering a more just and equitable society, the framing of racial dynamics as solely a product of power imbalances can obscure the complexities of racial relations.

Moreover, the propagation of identity politics and the politicization of race have led to the demonization of certain racial and ethnic groups, fostering resentment and division. Accusations of "reverse racism" and the vilification of individuals based on their race can exacerbate tensions and hinder efforts at reconciliation and understanding (*Chasing the Dream of Equity: How Policy Has Shaped Racial Economic Disparities*, 2023.).

Additionally, the rise of ethno-nationalism and the scapegoating of immigrant communities have further exacerbated ethnic tensions, as individuals are pitted against one another based on perceived differences. This divisive rhetoric undermines efforts at fostering unity and cohesion, perpetuating a cycle of animosity and mistrust that undermines efforts at building a more inclusive and equitable society (Presnall, 2020).

As our society grapples with the challenges of incivility, it's crucial to confront the deep-rooted divisions and tackle the underlying inequalities and injustices driving them. Only through nurturing empathy, understanding, and mutual respect can we aspire to construct a fairer, more inclusive society for everyone. To move forward collectively, we must resist fixating on past injustices as barriers to progress. It's time for national healing, without allowing divisive forces to further fracture our unity as Americans.

CHAPTER 5

CONSEQUENCES OF INCIVILITY

Erosion of Trust and Respect

One of the most profound consequences of incivility is the erosion of trust and respect within society. When individuals engage in uncivil behavior, whether online or in person, it undermines the foundational norms of mutual respect and empathy that are essential for fostering social cohesion. This erosion of trust extends beyond interpersonal relationships to institutions and societal structures, as citizens lose faith in the integrity and legitimacy of political leaders, media outlets, and public institutions.

Moreover, the erosion of trust and respect breeds cynicism and apathy, as individuals become disillusioned with the political process and disengaged from civic life (Citrin & Stoker, 2018). This disengagement further exacerbates divisions within society, as individuals retreat into their echo chambers and disengage from meaningful dialogue and collaboration.

Furthermore, the erosion of trust and respect undermines efforts at fostering cooperation and compromise, as individuals become increasingly entrenched in their perspectives and unwilling to entertain alternative viewpoints. This polarization impedes progress on pressing social issues and undermines efforts at finding common ground and building consensus.

In today's society, the erosion of trust and respect is a consequence of widespread incivility. Civility, often considered the cornerstone of healthy social interactions, encompasses politeness, respect, and consideration for others. However, as incivility becomes more prevalent, it undermines these fundamental values, leading to a breakdown in trust and respect among individuals and within communities.

One of the primary repercussions of incivility is the loss of trust in institutions and societal norms. When individuals witness or experience disrespectful behavior, whether in person or online, it breeds skepticism and cynicism towards authority figures, government institutions, and even traditional values. This erosion of trust can have far-reaching implications, affecting everything from political engagement to public safety.

Moreover, incivility fosters an environment where disrespect becomes normalized, leading to a vicious cycle of negativity and hostility. When individuals feel justified in expressing rudeness or contempt towards others, it creates a toxic atmosphere where healthy dialogue and cooperation are stifled. This breakdown in communication further exacerbates the erosion of trust, as meaningful connections become increasingly rare in a society plagued by incivility.

Furthermore, the erosion of trust and respect can have profound effects on mental health and well-being. Constant exposure to incivility, whether in personal interactions or through media channels, can contribute to feelings of isolation, anxiety, and depression. When individuals feel undervalued or disrespected, it can erode their sense of self-worth and belonging, further perpetuating the cycle of incivility.

In order to address the erosion of trust and respect in society, it is essential to promote civility as a core value in all aspects of life. This includes fostering empathy, promoting active listening, and encouraging constructive dialogue even in the face of disagreement. By prioritizing respect and understanding, we can begin to rebuild trust and create a more harmonious and inclusive society for future generations.

Threats to Democracy and Social Cohesion

The rise of incivility presents significant challenges to democracy and social unity, undermining the foundations of a healthy society. At the core of democracy lies the principle of respectful debate and the peaceful exchange of ideas. However, incivility disrupts this process by replacing reasoned discourse with hostility and aggression, ultimately eroding trust in democratic institutions and diminishing social cohesion (Vanderbilt, 2021).

One of the primary consequences of incivility is the polarization of society along ideological lines. When individuals resort to uncivil behavior, such as personal attacks or demonizing opponents, it deepens divisions within communities and reinforces an "us versus them" mentality. This polarization not only hampers meaningful dialogue but also undermines the ability of democratic institutions to address complex societal challenges.

Furthermore, incivility breeds distrust in political processes and institutions, leading to a loss of faith in the democratic system. When individuals feel that their voices are disregarded or disrespected, they may disengage from the political process altogether, further weakening democratic norms and institutions. This erosion of trust can have serious ramifications for the functioning of democracy, as citizens become disillusioned with the ability of elected officials to represent their interests.

Additionally, incivility can exacerbate social unrest and undermine social cohesion by fostering an atmosphere of fear and hostility. When individuals experience threats or marginalization due to uncivil behavior, it can lead to social fragmentation and a breakdown of community bonds. This fragmentation not only weakens the social fabric but also complicates efforts to address shared challenges and promote collective action.

To address the threats posed by incivility to democracy and social cohesion, it is imperative to promote civility as a fundamental value in public discourse and interpersonal interactions. This entails fostering empathy, encouraging active listening, and promoting respectful dialogue even amidst disagreement. By prioritizing civility, we can help rebuild trust in democratic institutions and strengthen the bonds that uphold society.

The Threat of Marxism, Socialism, and Communism

In recent years, the rise of incivility has been accompanied by a resurgence of ideologies such as Marxism, socialism, and communism, which pose significant threats to democracy and individual liberty. While these ideologies purport to promote social justice and equality, they often lead to authoritarianism, oppression, and economic stagnation.

Marxism, socialism, and communism advocate for the abolition of private property and the redistribution of wealth, promising to create a more equitable society. However, history has shown that these ideologies inevitably lead to centralized control, economic inefficiency, and the erosion of individual freedoms (Stephen, 2023a).

Moreover, the rise of Marxist-inspired movements such as critical race theory and intersectionality has further polarized society, fostering resentment and division along racial, gender, and class lines. By promoting the idea of collective guilt and victimhood, these ideologies undermine efforts at fostering empathy, understanding, and mutual respect.

The historical track record of Marxism, socialism, and communism is marred by numerous problems and failures that pose significant dangers to the current and future infrastructure of America. These ideologies have been associated with totalitarian regimes, human rights abuses, and economic stagnation. Examples such as the Soviet Union, Maoist China, and North Korea serve as stark reminders of the devastating consequences of implementing these systems.

One of the primary dangers of Marxism, socialism, and communism is the concentration of power in the hands of the state, leading to authoritarianism and the suppression of individual freedoms. These ideologies often prioritize collective interests over individual rights, resulting in censorship, political repression, and the persecution of dissenting voices. Such oppressive regimes undermine democratic principles and threaten the foundations of a free society.

Moreover, the economic policies advocated by Marxism, socialism, and communism have consistently failed to deliver prosperity and innovation. State control of the means of production stifles entrepreneurship and innovation, leading to inefficiency, shortages, and economic decline. Centralized planning and excessive government intervention in the economy distort market mechanisms, resulting in misallocation of resources and decreased productivity.

Additionally, the redistributionist nature of these ideologies can discourage hard work and initiative by disincentivizing success and rewarding mediocrity. When individuals are not adequately rewarded for their efforts, they may become demotivated, leading to a decline in productivity and economic growth. Furthermore, the reliance on government subsidies and welfare programs to achieve social equality can lead to unsustainable levels of debt and fiscal instability.

In summary, Marxism, socialism, and communism pose grave dangers to the current and future infrastructure of America. These ideologies have a history of oppressive governance, economic mismanagement, and social upheaval. By prioritizing state control over individual liberty and free markets, they undermine the principles of democracy and prosperity upon which America was founded. It is essential to remain vigilant against the allure of these ideologies and uphold the values of freedom, democracy, and capitalism.

Squatters Rights and the Invasion of Personal Property

The issue of squatter's rights laws and the invasion of homes and personal property poses significant problems in America, creating challenges for property owners, law enforcement, and the justice system. Squatter's rights, also known as adverse possession laws, allow individuals to claim ownership of property if they occupy it for a certain period of time without the owner's permission. While these laws were originally intended to prevent abandoned properties from falling into disrepair, they can be exploited by individuals seeking to gain ownership of occupied homes and land through illegitimate means.

One of the primary problems associated with squatter's rights laws is the potential for abuse and exploitation. In some cases, individuals may take advantage of loopholes in the law or exploit lax enforcement to occupy properties unlawfully. This can result in homeowners facing lengthy and costly legal battles to regain possession of their property, often with little recourse for recourse.

Furthermore, the invasion of homes and personal property by squatters can have serious consequences for property owners, including financial loss, emotional distress, and damage to their reputation and sense of security. Homeowners may find themselves unable to access or use their own property, facing harassment or intimidation from squatters, and dealing with the financial burden of legal fees and property damage.

Moreover, squatter's rights laws can create challenges for law enforcement and the justice system in addressing instances of illegal occupation. Determining rightful ownership of a property can be complex and time-consuming, requiring extensive investigation and legal proceedings. Meanwhile, squatters may exploit legal loopholes or delay tactics to prolong their unlawful occupation, further exacerbating the problem.

In addition to the immediate impact on property owners, the prevalence of squatter's rights laws and the invasion of homes and personal property can have broader societal implications. It undermines the rule of law and erodes public trust in the justice system, leading to a sense of injustice and disillusionment among affected individuals and communities. Furthermore, it can deter investment in real estate and economic development, as property owners may fear the risk of losing control of their assets to squatters.

In recent years, the surge of homelessness, illegal immigration, and the inability to accommodate the influx of individuals in our communities has contributed to a growing problem of squatters' rights and the invasion of personal property. As cities grapple with housing shortages and affordability crises, many individuals find themselves without a place to call home, leading to increased rates of homelessness and encampments in public spaces (Today, 2023).

Moreover, the rise of illegal immigration has further strained resources and exacerbated tensions in communities, as undocumented individuals seek shelter and support in areas already struggling to meet the needs of existing residents (Roy, 2022). This influx of individuals, coupled with limited resources and inadequate infrastructure, has created a perfect storm for conflict and contention over land use and property rights.

Furthermore, the entitled mindset of many individuals exacerbates the problem, as some individuals feel entitled to occupy public and private spaces without regard for the rights and interests of others. This sense of entitlement breeds resentment and animosity among those who feel their rights and freedoms are being infringed upon, leading to conflicts and confrontations in communities across the country.

The invasion of personal property and the erosion of property rights undermine the social contract that binds society together, fostering a climate of distrust and insecurity. When individuals feel their property rights are not being respected, it undermines the sense of stability and security that is essential for fostering social cohesion and trust.

As society grapples with the growing problem of squatters' rights and the invasion of personal property, it is imperative to address the root causes of homelessness, illegal immigration, and housing affordability crises. By investing in affordable housing, providing support services for vulnerable populations, and fostering a culture of empathy and compassion, we can create communities that are inclusive, equitable, and respectful of the rights and dignity of all individuals.

Mental Health Implications

The rise of incivility in America is accompanied by a range of mental health complications that have profound effects on individuals and society as a whole. Incivility, characterized by disrespectful behavior, hostility, and aggression, creates an environment of negativity and stress that can contribute to various mental health issues.

One of the primary mental health complications associated with increased incivility is heightened anxiety and stress. Constant exposure to rude or aggressive behavior, whether in personal interactions or through media channels, can trigger feelings of fear, unease, and insecurity. This chronic stress can take a toll on individuals' mental well-being, leading to symptoms such as irritability, sleep disturbances, and difficulty concentrating.

Moreover, incivility can fuel feelings of isolation and loneliness, exacerbating mental health problems such as depression. When individuals experience disrespect or hostility from others, it can erode their sense of belonging and connection to their community, leading to feelings of alienation and withdrawal. This social isolation can deepen feelings of despair and hopelessness, contributing to the onset or worsening of depressive symptoms.

Additionally, increased incivility can heighten feelings of anger and resentment, leading to interpersonal conflict and aggression. When individuals experience rudeness or disrespect from others, it can trigger defensive reactions and escalate confrontations, further perpetuating a cycle of incivility. This hostility in interpersonal relationships can strain social bonds and undermine trust, leading to feelings of betrayal and emotional distress.

Furthermore, the prevalence of incivility in public discourse and social media can contribute to a sense of moral distress and existential anxiety. Witnessing disrespectful behavior or engaging in heated debates online can leave individuals feeling morally compromised or disillusioned with society. This moral distress can lead to feelings of guilt, shame, and existential angst, as individuals grapple with their values and sense of integrity in the face of incivility.

The rise of incivility and polarization in society has profound implications for mental health, contributing to increased levels of stress, anxiety, and depression. When individuals are constantly exposed to vitriolic rhetoric and hostile interactions, it takes a toll on their psychological well-being, leading to feelings of isolation, hopelessness, and despair.

Moreover, the constant barrage of negative news and social media content can exacerbate feelings of helplessness and despair, as individuals become overwhelmed by the seemingly insurmountable challenges facing society. This sense of existential dread can lead to a loss of motivation and purpose, as individuals struggle to find meaning in an increasingly chaotic and hostile world.

Furthermore, the erosion of trust and social cohesion undermines the support networks and sense of community that are essential for maintaining mental health. When individuals feel disconnected and alienated from their peers, it exacerbates feelings of loneliness and isolation, leading to increased rates of depression and suicide.

As society grapples with the consequences of incivility, it is imperative to recognize the profound implications for mental health and well-being. By fostering empathy, understanding, and mutual respect, we can create a more compassionate and inclusive society that promotes the flourishing of all its members.

CHAPTER 6

STRATEGIES FOR RESTORING CIVILITY

How Do We Restore Civility?

Restoring civility requires a comprehensive approach that addresses the underlying causes of incivility while promoting empathy, understanding, and respect. One effective strategy is to create opportunities for meaningful engagement between individuals of diverse backgrounds. For example, community forums, town hall meetings, and interfaith dialogues provide platforms for individuals to come together, share their perspectives, and find common ground. By fostering spaces for dialogue and cooperation, communities can build bridges across divides and cultivate a culture of civility.

To genuinely foster civility, we must engage in challenging conversations and confront difficult truths with a commitment to positive transformation. Although some may react with anger and defensiveness to what I'm about to say, it remains a truth we cannot ignore. Until we can openly discuss these issues without immediately resorting to defensive responses, efforts to promote civility will continue to falter.

The reality is that individuals, regardless of their skin color or ethnicity, can hold and exhibit racist beliefs and behaviors toward those who differ from them. This means that racism exists within all racial and ethnic groups. It's important to clarify that not everyone within these groups espouses racist views, but it's undeniable that racism permeates various communities (Pew Research Center, 2021). If we're unwilling to acknowledge this fundamental truth, then any calls for civility are bound to be ineffective. Thus, our starting point must be an acknowledgment and understanding of human imperfection, recognizing that injustices occur across ethnic, religious, and societal lines without discrimination. We must initiate a dialogue aimed at dismantling the pervasive falsehood that labels all white individuals as inherently privileged, oppressive, racist, and inherently dangerous beings. Similarly, we must challenge the narrative that categorizes all black individuals as criminals and perpetual victims of microaggressions. This dialogue is essential for fostering understanding, empathy, and ultimately, reconciliation within our society.

In addition to promoting interpersonal dialogue, restoring civility also involves addressing systemic barriers to understanding and cooperation. This may include implementing policies that promote diversity, equity, and inclusion in workplaces, schools, and other institutions. By creating environments that value and celebrate diversity, communities can foster a sense of belonging and respect for all individuals, regardless of their background or identity.

Furthermore, restoring civility requires a commitment to promoting ethical leadership and responsible citizenship. Leaders at all levels of society have a responsibility to model civility and respect in their words and actions. By holding leaders accountable for their behavior and promoting a culture of integrity and accountability, communities can cultivate a culture of civility and respect that permeates all aspects of society.

Promoting Empathy and Active Listening

Promoting empathy and active listening is essential for restoring civility and building meaningful connections between individuals. One effective strategy is to incorporate empathy-building exercises into educational curricula and workplace training programs. For example, role-playing scenarios and perspective-taking activities can help individuals develop a deeper understanding of others' experiences and perspectives.

Furthermore, promoting media literacy is crucial for equipping individuals with the skills and knowledge necessary to navigate the complexities of the modern information landscape. By teaching individuals how to critically evaluate media content and identify sources of misinformation, communities can empower individuals to engage with media content in a responsible and discerning manner.

Additionally, fostering empathy and active listening requires creating spaces for dialogue and conversation where individuals feel safe and respected. This may include organizing community forums, discussion groups, and storytelling events where individuals can share their experiences and perspectives in a supportive environment. By providing opportunities for individuals to listen to and learn from one another, communities can foster empathy, understanding, and respect.

Fostering Constructive Dialogue

Fostering constructive dialogue requires creating environments where individuals feel empowered to engage in respectful and productive conversations, even when they disagree. One effective strategy is to establish ground rules for communication that emphasize mutual respect, active listening, and a commitment to finding common ground. By setting clear expectations for civil discourse, communities can create spaces where individuals feel safe to express their opinions and constructively engage with others.

Furthermore, fostering constructive dialogue involves promoting the value of diversity and inclusion in all aspects of society. This may include implementing policies and practices that promote diversity in leadership, decision-making, and representation. By ensuring that diverse voices are heard and valued, communities can foster a culture of inclusion and respect that enriches public discourse and promotes understanding.

Additionally, fostering constructive dialogue requires a commitment to addressing systemic barriers to participation and representation. This may include providing resources and support for marginalized communities to participate in public life and decision-making processes. By promoting equity and inclusion, communities can ensure that all individuals have a voice in shaping the future of their communities.

Advocating for Christianity in America: Making America Civil Again

Advocating for Christianity in America can play a significant role in restoring civility and promoting values of love, compassion, and forgiveness. One effective strategy is to engage in community outreach and service projects that demonstrate the transformative power of faith in action. For example, religious organizations can organize food drives, homeless shelters, and disaster relief efforts to address the needs of vulnerable populations and promote social justice.

Furthermore, advocating for Christianity in America involves promoting the importance of faith and morality in public life. This may include advocating for policies and initiatives that align with Christian values, such as promoting the sanctity of life, protecting religious freedom, and supporting families and communities. By actively participating in the public square and advocating for policies that reflect Christian principles, communities can promote a culture of civility and respect for all individuals.

Additionally, advocating for Christianity in America requires a commitment to fostering interfaith dialogue and cooperation. By building bridges with individuals of other faiths and promoting mutual understanding and respect, communities can cultivate a culture of inclusivity and cooperation that transcends religious differences. By working together to address common challenges and promote shared values, communities can foster a culture of civility and respect that reflects the teachings of Christianity.

An anti-Christian progressive liberal once told me that America's forefathers were all Deists. She expressed frustration & contempt that I did not agree with her. As modern culture attempts to rewrite history, sanity & truth must prevail. A deist is a person who believes in the existence of a higher power or creator but does not follow a specific religious doctrine or believe in divine intervention in human affairs. Deists generally rely on reason and observation of the natural world to understand the existence and nature of God (Pailin & Manuel, 2024).

Jamestown, Virginia is known for being the first permanent English settlement in North America, established in 1607. The church played a significant role in the early colonization of America and the spread of Christianity in the region. Historians and archaeologists have relied on various sources and methods to build the replica of the church in Jamestown, Virginia. This includes archaeological excavations, historical documents, paintings, comparative analysis, etc. to construct the replica of that church that stands today as a tourist attraction (Mullen, 2023).

In March 2017, I stood in that church replica. As I entered the front door, turned, and faced the right rear wall, there hung a sign shown in this photograph. I saw it with my own eyes. We took many photos of the building, especially that sign (see picture below), and inquired about the accuracy of that sign being there. The tour guide affirmed it's there because the diaries and other historical writings of the church in Jamestown show that it was there in the original building. Go see it for yourself. Simply, this conflicts with the progressive liberal antichrist argument that early Americans had no specific faith. It's clear they did & that they preached & believed Acts 2:38. They were Christian and preached repentance of sin, water baptism in the name of Jesus Christ, and being filled with the Holy Ghost (Curtis, 2018). That's not Deism. That's Apostolic.

Despite the efforts of certain interest groups to erase Christianity from the fabric of America, historical evidence unequivocally confirms that the majority of our founding fathers identified as Christian (Holmes, 2006). Throughout generations, Americans have upheld traditional Christian values that resonate with the teachings of the Bible. Christianity has permeated various aspects of our society, including our education system, interpersonal relationships, work ethic, business practices, and core values.

It's essential to recognize that Christians, like adherents of other faiths such as Scientologists and Atheists, are not immune to imperfection. However, it's also nothing new that voices opposing Christianity often dominate mainstream media channels and are amplified by pop culture icons. The Bible itself warns us, in the book of 1 John, that in the last days, many anti-Christ figures will emerge as prominent voices in our world.

I hold deep admiration for Coleman Hughes, an African American author renowned for his book "The End of Race Politics: Arguments for a Colorblind America" (Panreck, 2024). His perspective resonates with mine, advocating for a vision of an America free from the constraints of race and the cessation of deliberate race-driven provocations. Recently, Hughes was extended an invitation to appear on "The View" to discuss his book. However, the conversation took a contentious turn when Sunny Hostin, one of the hosts, labeled him a charlatan, suggesting that he is disconnected from the black community. Furthermore, she insinuated that he might have received compensation from Republican interests to promote his viewpoints (Panreck, 2024).

This is a classic example of how the media unconscionably engages in race-baiting and race politics. Millions of viewers are exposed to extreme and faulty ideologies like this, and the world becomes less civil as a result. Imagine a world where we unconditionally love, value, and respect each other as human beings without regard to skin pigmentation or ethnicity. What a world that would be!

Over the past couple of decades, America has become an increasingly anti-Christian nation. It's true. Christian church attendance and affiliation are experiencing a rapid decline (Mitchell, 2020). What happened? More importantly, why is this happening? Is there any correlation between the increased incivility in our nation and the decline of Christianity? I think there is sufficient evidence to show a strong correlation.

In recent years, Christianity in America has faced a notable decline for several reasons. Firstly, there's been a cultural shift towards secularism and skepticism, particularly among younger generations, leading to a decreased adherence to religious beliefs and practices. Secondly, scandals within religious institutions, including cases of abuse and financial impropriety, have eroded trust in organized religion, causing some individuals to disassociate themselves from church communities (Gabbatt, 2023). Thirdly, advancements in science and technology have challenged traditional religious narratives, with some people finding it difficult to reconcile ancient religious teachings with modern scientific understanding. Fourthly, the rise of individualism and consumerism has fostered a culture of self-gratification and materialism, drawing people away from spiritual pursuits and towards material comforts. Finally, societal changes such as increased diversity and globalization have exposed individuals to a wider array of belief systems and worldviews, prompting some to question the exclusivity of Christianity and explore alternative spiritual paths (Cohen, 2022).

These factors collectively contribute to the ongoing decline of Christianity's influence and prominence in American society.

We must learn the art of respectful disagreement without vilifying those who hold differing views. Community, choices, conscience, and character are all integral aspects of civility. It transcends mere politeness, encompassing the cultivation of a civil disposition and a sense of civil responsibility. Through civility, deeper and more meaningful friendships and relationships often emerge, infused with a sense of civic duty that extends beyond individual interests.

In Mark 12:30-31, Jesus Christ imparts profound wisdom, emphasizing the paramount importance of loving God with our entire being and treating others with the same kindness and respect we desire for ourselves. This directive encapsulates the essence of civility. Indeed, there is no greater display of civility than demonstrating love and respect towards others simply because it aligns with the principles of righteousness.

"Blessed is the nation whose God is the Lord" is a profound declaration found in Psalm 33:12 of the King James Version of the Bible. This verse highlights the foundational importance of acknowledging God as the ultimate authority and source of blessing for a nation. When a nation embraces God and aligns its principles and governance with His will, it experiences His favor, guidance, and protection. Conversely, when a nation rejects God and turns away from His precepts, it risks facing the consequences of its disobedience. In this perspective, a nation that rejects God may experience moral decay, societal unrest, and ultimately, divine judgment. Just as blessings follow obedience, so do consequences follow disobedience, illustrating the vital role of acknowledging God in the affairs of nations.

If America has any hope of the restoration of civility and peace, it must look to our roots and embrace our Christian heritage once again. The rise of anti-Christian sentiments, ideals, and behaviors has made America increasingly less civil and less safe. The fabric of our society has eroded and paved the way for increased rage, crime, immorality, and incivility. Do you want to help fix this issue? Go to Google.com. Type in, *"ALJC churches near me"* or *"Find an Apostolic Pentecostal Church Nearby"*. Visit one of those churches and find one that you feel comfortable making your home church. Bring your children to Sunday School and regularly scheduled church services. Read the Bible and begin embodying its teachings. Start a prayer life and teach your family how to pray. Obey Acts 2:38 which calls for everyone to repent of sin, be baptized in the name of Jesus Christ, and be filled with the Holy Ghost. Little by little, things will change in a positive and meaningful way. We can reclaim this great nation from those who have hijacked it and made it a warzone of violence and incivility.

CHAPTER 7

CASE STUDIES AND SUCCESS STORIES

Community Initiatives and Grassroots Movements

Community initiatives and grassroots movements have played a crucial role in restoring civility and promoting dialogue and cooperation within communities. One example of a successful community initiative is the "Neighborhood Circles" program in Seattle, Washington. This program brings together residents from diverse backgrounds to discuss issues affecting their community, build relationships, and work together to address common challenges (Rights, 2023). Through open and respectful dialogue, participants have been able to find common ground and develop creative solutions to issues such as homelessness, crime, and public safety.

Similarly, grassroots movements such as the "Better Angels" organization have been successful in bringing together individuals from across the political spectrum to engage in constructive dialogue and bridge divides (Thompson, 2018). Through workshops, town hall meetings, and community events, Better Angels provides a space for individuals to listen to and learn from one another, even when they disagree. By focusing on common values and shared goals, participants can find areas of agreement and build relationships based on mutual respect and understanding.

Moreover, community-based organizations such as the "Faith in Action" network have been successful in mobilizing communities to address social issues and promote social justice (*Faith in Action (Formerly PICO National Network)*, 2020). By bringing together individuals from diverse faith traditions, Faith in Action provides a platform for collective action and advocacy on issues such as affordable housing, healthcare, and immigration reform. Through grassroots organizing and community engagement, Faith in Action empowers individuals to make a difference in their communities and build a more just and equitable society.

Community initiatives and grassroots movements play a crucial role in restoring civility and promoting dialogue and cooperation within communities. By providing spaces for individuals to come together, share their perspectives, and work together towards common goals, these initiatives foster a culture of civility and respect that enriches public discourse and strengthens social bonds.

Examples of Effective Leadership

Effective leadership is essential for restoring civility and promoting cooperation and dialogue within communities. One example of effective leadership is the "Courageous Conversations" program in Montgomery County, Maryland. Led by county executive Marc Elrich, Courageous Conversations brings together community leaders, elected officials, and residents to discuss issues of race, equity, and inclusion (Stricklin, 2019). Through facilitated dialogue and storytelling, participants can explore their own biases and assumptions, challenge stereotypes, and develop a deeper understanding of one another's experiences.

Similarly, effective leadership at the national level has been demonstrated by organizations such as the "National Institute for Civil Discourse" (NICD) (National Institute for Civil Discourse, 2023). Founded in the aftermath of the 2011 shooting in Tucson, Arizona, that injured congresswoman Gabrielle Giffords, NICD works to promote civility and respect in public discourse. Through research, education, and advocacy, NICD provides resources and support for elected officials, community leaders, and citizens to engage in constructive dialogue and bridge divides.

Moreover, effective leadership within religious communities has been demonstrated by organizations such as the "Interfaith Youth Core" (IFYC) (Sector, 2022). Founded by Eboo Patel, IFYC works to promote interfaith cooperation and understanding among young people. Through programs such as the "Better Together" campaign, IFYC empowers young people to bridge religious divides, engage in dialogue, and work together to address pressing social issues.

In conclusion, effective leadership is essential for restoring civility and promoting cooperation and dialogue within communities. By fostering a culture of respect, empathy, and understanding, leaders can create spaces for individuals to come together, share their perspectives, and work towards common goals.

How We Can All Help Restore Civility

While effective leadership and community initiatives play a crucial role in restoring civility, individual actions also have a significant impact. One way that individuals can help restore civility is by modeling respectful and empathetic behavior in their own interactions with others. By practicing active listening, seeking to understand differing perspectives, and treating others with kindness and respect, individuals can create a culture of civility in their own communities.

Furthermore, individuals can contribute to restoring civility by actively participating in community initiatives and grassroots movements. Whether by volunteering their time, attending community meetings, or participating in dialogue and advocacy efforts, individuals can make a difference in their communities and contribute to positive social change.

Moreover, individuals can help restore civility by educating themselves and others about the importance of civil discourse and respectful dialogue. By learning about the root causes of incivility and the impact of divisive rhetoric, individuals can become more informed and engaged citizens, better equipped to promote understanding and cooperation within their communities.

However, that doesn't excuse any of us from using the "race card" to justify our actions and behavior. Until our nation moves past dwelling on past injustices and using them as justifications for expectations, actions, and behavior, true healing won't occur. Reparations cannot and will not heal our nation. It's not fair to penalize individuals who were never slaveowners to pay restitution for crimes and injustices they never committed. Slavery was abolished over 160 years ago, and there isn't a person alive in America today who has ever been a slave owner or a slave. Carrying generational baggage into the future hinders our nation from healing and coming together. The solution is simple, yet many choose to reject it. We must love one another without regard to color and recognize that there is only one race—the human race.

In conclusion, restoring civility requires a collective effort from individuals, communities, and leaders at all levels of society. By modeling respectful behavior, participating in community initiatives, and educating themselves and others about the importance of civil discourse, individuals can contribute to building a more inclusive, respectful, and empathetic society.

CHAPTER 8

THE ROLE OF INDIVIDUALS IN CONFRONTING CHAOS

In the quest to confront chaos and restore civility, the role of individuals cannot be overstated. Each person has the power to make a difference through their actions, attitudes, and interactions with others. This chapter delves into the various ways that individuals can play a pivotal role in addressing the challenges of incivility and building a more harmonious society.

Taking Personal Responsibility

At the heart of confronting chaos lies the concept of personal responsibility. Each individual must recognize their role in shaping the culture of their community and take ownership of their actions and behaviors. This entails reflecting on one's conduct and considering how it contributes to either the perpetuation or alleviation of incivility.

Taking personal responsibility involves making conscious choices to prioritize respect, empathy, and understanding in all interactions. It means acknowledging when one has acted in a manner inconsistent with these values and taking steps to rectify any harm caused. By holding ourselves accountable for our actions, we set a positive example for others and contribute to the collective effort to restore civility.

Thinking for One's Self Rather than Adopting Cultural and Trending Norms

In a world influenced by cultural and trending norms, individuals must cultivate the ability to think critically and independently. Rather than blindly conforming to societal expectations or following the latest trends, individuals should exercise discernment and question prevailing attitudes and beliefs.

Thinking for oneself involves examining issues from multiple perspectives, seeking out reliable sources of information, and forming opinions based on evidence and reasoned analysis. It requires the courage to challenge conventional wisdom and the humility to admit when one's views may need revision in light of new information (Southworth, 2022).

By thinking for themselves, individuals can resist the polarizing effects of echo chambers and filter bubbles, where like-minded individuals reinforce each other's biases. Instead, they can engage in constructive dialogue with those who hold different viewpoints, fostering mutual understanding and respect.

Treat Others as You Want to Be Treated

The age-old adage "treat others as you want to be treated" remains as relevant as ever in the quest to restore civility. This principle, often referred to as the Golden Rule, emphasizes the importance of empathy and reciprocity in human interactions.

By treating others with kindness, dignity, and respect, individuals cultivate a culture of civility and contribute to the well-being of their communities. This means listening attentively to others, valuing their perspectives, and refraining from resorting to personal attacks or derogatory language.

Moreover, the Golden Rule encourages individuals to consider the impact of their words and actions on others and strive to minimize harm. It serves as a guiding principle for resolving conflicts and fostering reconciliation, reminding individuals of their shared humanity and interconnectedness.

Cultivating a Culture of Respect

Central to the restoration of civility is the cultivation of a culture of respect within communities. This involves recognizing and valuing the inherent worth and dignity of every individual, regardless of their background, beliefs, or identity.

Cultivating a culture of respect begins with fostering empathy and understanding towards others. It means actively seeking to learn about different cultures, experiences, and perspectives, and celebrating the diversity that enriches our communities.

Furthermore, cultivating a culture of respect requires individuals to challenge prejudice, discrimination, and injustice wherever they encounter it. It involves speaking out against bigotry and intolerance and advocating for the rights and dignity of all individuals. By cultivating a culture of respect, individuals can create communities where everyone feels valued, included, and respected, laying the foundation for constructive dialogue and cooperation.

Building Bridges Across Divides

In a society characterized by polarization and division, building bridges across divides is essential for restoring civility and promoting unity. This requires individuals to reach out to those who hold different viewpoints, engage in respectful dialogue, and seek common ground.

Building bridges involves finding areas of agreement and shared values, even amidst disagreement. It requires a willingness to listen with an open mind, acknowledge the validity of others' perspectives, and work towards mutually beneficial solutions.

Moreover, building bridges across divides requires individuals to transcend their own biases and preconceptions and approach interactions with humility and curiosity. It involves recognizing the humanity in others and seeking to build connections based on empathy, understanding, and respect.

By building bridges across divides, individuals can break down barriers, foster mutual trust, and create a sense of belonging and unity within their communities. This collaborative approach is essential for addressing the complex challenges facing society and building a more inclusive and harmonious future.

In conclusion, the role of individuals in confronting chaos and restoring civility cannot be overstated. Through taking personal responsibility, thinking critically, treating others with respect, cultivating a culture of empathy, and building bridges across divides, individuals can contribute to the collective effort to build a more harmonious and inclusive society.

CHAPTER 9

NAVIGATING GENDER IDENTITY FROM A CONSERVATIVE CHRISTIAN PERSPECTIVE

Let me begin this chapter with a statement of truth that holds profound importance: You and I don't have to see eye to eye on the issue of gender identity to love and respect each other. As a conservative Christian, I hold firm to my faith and the Biblical belief in only two biological genders: male and female. However, if you believe in multiple genders and I don't agree with you, it doesn't mean I harbor hatred towards you or am violating your human rights.

Imagine if I demanded that everyone in the world be a Christian—would that be acceptable? Would you welcome that without resistance? This is not an apples-and-oranges type of debate. The belief in multiple genders doesn't align with biological science or other scientific principles. It's a social trend that's gaining popularity, but lacks scientific support. Therefore, in many ways, transgenderism can be likened to a type of religion.

Consider this: it requires a significant amount of belief and convincing for a biological male to look in the mirror and see himself as female. Similarly, it takes belief and convincing for biological females to accept biological males identifying as females in their restrooms and locker rooms. Just as I shouldn't impose my religious beliefs on you, you shouldn't impose your ideologies on me and others. Your beliefs are your own, and it's not fair to enforce them on others or react angrily when others don't share the same views. We can respectfully agree to disagree without resorting to incivility.

Still not convinced? Let me approach it from a different angle. Transgenderism encompasses a wide range of sexual orientations, but it often overlooks or excludes those who identify as heterosexual and are comfortable with their biological gender. Despite claiming to promote inclusion, transgenderism can be seen as exclusive in this regard.

None of the sexual orientations under the transgender umbrella are supported by scientific evidence. Therefore, embracing these ideologies requires individuals to believe in something that cannot be proven or observed. In this sense, transgenderism can be likened to a form of religion.

Just as you have the right to practice your religion, others have the same right. However, this doesn't give anyone the authority to impose their beliefs on others. Each person should be free to hold their own beliefs without coercion or societal pressure from others.

The issue of gender identity has become a contentious topic in modern society, particularly among conservative Christians who hold steadfast to traditional beliefs. This chapter delves into the challenges faced by conservative Christians in navigating changing societal norms around gender identity while upholding their deeply held beliefs and values.

Upholding Traditional Values

Conservative Christians have long adhered to traditional beliefs about gender, rooted in biblical teachings that affirm the binary nature of gender as male and female. These beliefs are deeply ingrained in their faith and worldview, shaping their understanding of identity, relationships, and societal roles.

In the face of changing cultural norms that embrace a spectrum of gender identities, conservative Christians must remain steadfast in upholding their traditional values. This means affirming the biblical definition of gender while resisting pressures to conform to secular ideologies that undermine their faith.

Conservative Christians often uphold traditional norms of biological gender, rooted in their interpretation of biblical teachings and cultural values. For many conservative Christians, the belief in the binary understanding of gender as male and female is deeply ingrained in their religious convictions. They view gender as an essential aspect of God's design, with distinct roles and responsibilities assigned to men and women.

In conservative Christian communities, there is often an emphasis on the complementarity of the sexes, where men and women are seen as equal in value but distinct in their God-given roles. This perspective is informed by biblical passages that outline specific gender roles within the family, church, and society. For example, passages such as Ephesians 5:22-33 and Titus 2:3-5 are often cited to support the idea of husbands as leaders and providers within the family and wives as nurturers and helpers.

Furthermore, conservative Christians uphold traditional norms of biological gender through their views on sexuality and marriage. They typically affirm heterosexual relationships as the biblical norm, based on passages such as Genesis 2:24 and Matthew 19:4-6, which describe marriage as a union between one man and one woman. This perspective leads conservative Christians to advocate for policies and laws that uphold the sanctity of marriage and protect religious freedom for individuals and organizations that adhere to traditional views of sexuality and gender.

In recent years, conservative Christians have become increasingly vocal in their opposition to movements and ideologies that challenge traditional norms of biological gender, such as gender fluidity and transgenderism. They view these movements as contrary to biblical teaching and harmful to individuals and society. Instead, conservative Christians advocate for a return to biblical principles and traditional values regarding gender, which they believe offer the best framework for understanding human identity and relationships.

Navigating Conflicting Perspectives

As modern culture increasingly embraces diverse gender identities, conservative Christians find themselves at odds with prevailing societal norms. The concept of gender fluidity and nonbinary identities challenges their traditional beliefs, leading to tensions and conflicts within communities and families (Twenge, 2023).

Conservative Christians must navigate these conflicting perspectives with grace and civility, recognizing the importance of respecting individuals' autonomy while also upholding their own beliefs. This requires engaging in dialogue with compassion and empathy, even when faced with disagreement or opposition.

As society increasingly embraces a transgender perspective, conservative Christians are faced with the challenge of upholding their biblical beliefs while navigating the complexities of a changing cultural landscape. For many conservative Christians, the concept of transgenderism conflicts with their understanding of God's design for gender and human identity as outlined in the Bible. This tension can lead to complications in conversations and interactions with individuals who identify as transgender, as well as broader societal debates about gender identity and expression.

One of the main complications conservative Christians face is the clash between their religious convictions and societal norms regarding gender identity. As society becomes more accepting of transgender individuals and advocates for greater recognition and protection of their rights, conservative Christians may feel marginalized or pressured to compromise their beliefs. They may encounter challenges in expressing their views on gender and sexuality in public discourse, facing accusations of bigotry or intolerance for adhering to traditional biblical teachings.

Furthermore, conservative Christians may struggle with how to engage with transgender individuals respectfully and compassionately while remaining faithful to their convictions. They may wrestle with questions about how to affirm the dignity and worth of all individuals, including those who identify as transgender, while also upholding their understanding of biblical truth. This tension can lead to uncertainty and discomfort in conversations about gender identity and expression.

Moreover, conservative Christians may feel that it is unfair for the transgender community to impose their ideologies on those whose faith does not support it. They may perceive efforts to promote transgender rights and inclusion as infringing upon their religious freedom and autonomy to live according to their beliefs. This can lead to feelings of frustration and resentment, as conservative Christians navigate the tension between respecting the rights and dignity of transgender individuals and maintaining their religious convictions.

Embracing Tolerance and Civility

In a pluralistic society, tolerance and civility are essential virtues that must be embraced by all, regardless of ideological differences. While conservative Christians may hold firm to our beliefs about gender, we must also demonstrate respect and compassion towards those who hold differing views. That doesn't mean we have to agree with their views or that we endorse those views. It simply means we are choosing to be civil.

True tolerance means recognizing the dignity and worth of every individual, regardless of their beliefs or identities. Conservative Christians are called to love their neighbors as themselves, even when they disagree on matters of gender identity. This requires extending grace and kindness toward others, even as they stand firm in their convictions. Likewise, for civility to return and prevail, non-Christian groups must show mutual respect to conservative Christians in their values and beliefs. Hostility forms whenever demands to conform to a certain perspective overshadow individual choice and liberty. In other words, a biological male has the right to pretend to be a female if he so chooses but he does not have the right to force me to believe along with him. We all have a right to disagree with one another's perspectives and ideals. However, we must choose to do so with civility.

Promoting Biblical Principles

At the heart of the gender identity conflict lies the need to uphold biblical principles in navigating these complex issues.

Conservative Christians must turn to Scripture for guidance, seeking wisdom and discernment in addressing questions of gender and identity.

Biblical teachings affirm the inherent dignity and worth of every individual, emphasizing their creation in the image of God. While conservative Christians maintain a binary understanding of gender, they are called to demonstrate love, compassion, and respect towards all individuals, mirroring the compassionate example set forth by Jesus Christ. According to the Bible, the understanding is clear: there are two genders, male and female, as ordained by God. Should an individual choose to diverge from their biological framework, the U.S. Constitution grants them the freedom to do so. However, it is essential to note that while individuals have the right to their choices, they should not compel or demand others to conform to their beliefs. In other words, a transgender individual does not have the right to force Christians to embrace his or her chosen identity.

Navigating the gender identity conflict from a conservative Christian perspective requires upholding traditional values while embracing tolerance and civility towards those with differing beliefs. By grounding themselves in biblical principles and extending grace toward others, conservative Christians can engage in dialogue with humility and compassion, seeking to promote understanding and respect in a pluralistic society.

Wrapping up "Confronting Chaos: The Civility Crisis," we've explored the challenges of our modern world, confronting the decline of civility and the surge of conflict. From the political arena to our daily lives, we've seen how things are getting messy, often drowned out by loud arguments and sharp divides. But amidst this chaos, there's a glimmer of hope—a hope tied to our resilience as people and the enduring strength of compassion.

Navigating the complexities of the 21st century, it's evident that restoring civility requires collective effort and individual responsibility. It's about engaging in tough conversations, challenging our own biases, and extending empathy to those with whom we disagree. True civility isn't just about avoiding conflict; it's about showing respect, understanding, and a genuine commitment to dialogue. It's about choosing unity over division and prioritizing the common good over self-interest.

Amid the chaos, let's be the architects of civility—building bridges, listening, and showing kindness. By working together to confront chaos with civility, we pave the way for a more compassionate and harmonious world. So, as we embark on this journey, let's hold onto the belief that through our shared humanity, we can indeed confront chaos and create a brighter future.

ABOUT THE AUTHOR

Nelson Grimmett, a passionate advocate for harmony in an increasingly discordant world, brings a unique blend of wisdom and compassion to his writing. With a heart deeply rooted in faith and community, Nelson's journey toward understanding and addressing societal challenges has been a lifelong pursuit.

Drawing from his diverse roles as an Administrative Assistant at KCCU radio with Cameron University and as the Senior Pastor of Great Plains Apostolic Church in Lawton, Oklahoma, Nelson has gained invaluable insights into the complexities of human interaction. Through his work, he has witnessed firsthand the transformative power of empathy and dialogue in navigating even the most turbulent of times.

"Confronting Chaos: The Civility Crisis" reflects Nelson's unwavering commitment to fostering respect and understanding amidst chaos. In this book, he explores the profound importance of civility in our everyday lives, offering practical guidance and heartfelt reflections on how we can bridge divides and cultivate a culture of kindness and cooperation.

Beyond his professional endeavors, Nelson finds solace and inspiration in the simple joys of life: a warm cup of coffee, the companionship of his beloved dogs, and the timeless wisdom found in the pages of a good book. His love for storytelling, coupled with a deep reverence for the written Word of God, infuses his writing with authenticity and warmth.

With a vision for a more harmonious world and a dedication to spreading positivity wherever he goes, Nelson Grimmett invites readers on a journey of self-reflection, growth, and the pursuit of common ground. Through his words, he reminds us that, even amid chaos, there is always hope for a brighter tomorrow.

BIBLIOGRAPHY

Admin, R. (2018, October 25). *The rise of incivility in America - Ray Williams.* Ray Williams. https://raywilliams.ca/the-rise-of-incivility-in-america/

Author, N. (2020, May 30). *Millennials: Confident. connected. open to change | Pew Research Center.* Pew Research Center's Social & Demographic Trends Project. https://www.pewresearch.org/social-trends/2010/02/24/millennials-confident-connected-open-to-change/

Barberá, P. (2020, September 1). *Social media, echo chambers, and political polarization.* Cambridge Core. https://www.cambridge.org/core/books/social-media-and-democracy/social-media-echo-chambers-and-political-polarization/333A5B4DE1B67EFF7876261118CCFE19

Barneclo, M. (2021, May 23). *It's Time to Stop Blindly Idolizing Celebrities.* The UCSD Guardian. https://ucsdguardian.org/2021/05/23/its-time-to-stop-blindly-idolizing-celebrities/

Bentley University. (2015, June 2). Millennials and the Power of Changing Perceptions | Bentley University. *Bentley University.* https://www.bentley.edu/news/millennials-and-power-changing-perceptions

Beshay. (2023, July 13). *Support for the Black Lives Matter movement has dropped considerably from its peak in 2020 | Pew Research Center.* Pew Research Center's Social & Demographic Trends Project. https://www.pewresearch.org/social-trends/2023/06/14/support-for-the-black-lives-matter-movement-has-dropped-considerably-from-its-peak-in-2020/

BlackPast. (2019, September 23). *(1963) Malcolm X, "Racial Separation"* • https://www.blackpast.org/african-american-history/speeches-african-american-history/1963-malcolm-x-racial-separation/#:~:text=On%20October%2011%2C%201963%2C%20Malcolm%20X%20gave%20a,best%20approach%20to%20the%20problems%20facing%20black%20America.

Can Historic Social Injustices be Addressed Through Reparations? (2022, August 31). Harvard Business Review. https://hbr.org/podcast/2021/03/can-historic-social-injustices-be-addressed-through-reparations

Chambre, H., & McLellan, D. T. (2024, January 23). *Marxism | Definition, History, Ideology, Examples, & Facts.* Encyclopedia Britannica. https://www.britannica.com/topic/Marxism

Chasing the dream of equity: How policy has shaped racial economic disparities. (2023, August 1). Economic Policy Institute. https://www.epi.org/publication/chasing-the-dream-of-equity/

Childers, T. (2019, October 23). *Green Bank Observatory: Pioneering Radio Astronomy.* Space.com. https://www.space.com/green-bank-observatory.html

Citrin, J., & Stoker, L. (2018). Political trust in a cynical age. *Annual Review of Political Science, 21*(1), 49–70. https://doi.org/10.1146/annurev-polisci-050316-092550

Cohen, L. (2022, September 14). Christianity in the U.S. is quickly shrinking and may no longer be the majority religion within just a few decades, research finds. *CBS News.* https://www.cbsnews.com/news/christianity-us-shrinking-pew-research/

Communist Party (united States) | Encyclopedia.com. (2016, August 24). https://www.encyclopedia.com/history/united-states-and-canada/us-history/communist-party-united-states

Curtis, K., PhD. (2018, March 5). *Christianity in Jamestown.* Christianity.com. https://www.christianity.com/church/church-history/timeline/1601-1700/christianity-in-jamestown-11630060.html

Davidai, S., & Ongis, M. (2019). The politics of zero-sum thinking: The relationship between political ideology and the belief that life is a zero-sum game. *Science Advances, 5*(12). https://doi.org/10.1126/sciadv.aay3761

Davis, S. (2018, June 25). Congressional leaders criticize Maxine Waters for urging confrontation. *NPR*. https://www.npr.org/2018/06/25/623206039/congressional-leaders-criticize-maxine-waters-for-urging-confrontation

Faith in Action (Formerly PICO National Network). (2020, October 4). The Pluralism Project. https://pluralism.org/pico-national-network

Fleming, A. (2020, April 2). Why social media makes us so angry, and what you can do about it. BBC Science Focus Magazine. https://www.sciencefocus.com/the-human-body/why-social-media-makes-us-so-angry-and-what-you-can-do-about-it

Gabbatt, A. (2023, January 23). Losing their religion: why US churches are on the decline. *The Guardian*. https://www.theguardian.com/us-news/2023/jan/22/us-churches-closing-religion-covid-christianity

Gonzalez, M. (2022, November 14). *How cultural Marxism threatens the United States—and how Americans can fight it | The Heritage Foundation*. The Heritage Foundation. https://www.heritage.org/progressivism/report/how-cultural-marxism-threatens-the-united-states-and-how-americans-can-fight

Grossman, H. (2024a, February 7). "Woke Kindergarten" teacher calls for destruction of America: "We've been trying to end y'all." *Fox News*. https://www.foxnews.com/media/public-school-consultant-calls-destruction-america-trying-end-yall

Grossman, H. (2024b, March 13). Maryland city equity official says she wants US to burn to the ground: "MY ideology can rise from the ashes." *Fox News*. https://www.foxnews.com/media/maryland-city-equity-official-says-wants-us-burn-ground-ideology-rise-ashes

Grossman, H. (2024c, March 20). UN secretary-general youth climate adviser calls for Whites to be stripped of power in "revolutionary fights." *Fox News*. https://www.foxnews.com/media/un-secretary-generals-climate-adviser-calls-white-stripped-power-revolutionary-fights

Hall, A. (2024, March 22). Carville advises Biden to have others do his "wet work" against Trump: "Take a guy out." *Fox News*. https://www.foxnews.com/media/carville-advises-biden-others-wet-work-against-trump-take-guy-out

Hall, J., & Leary, M. (2024, February 20). *The U.S. has an empathy deficit.* Scientific American. https://www.scientificamerican.com/article/the-us-has-an-empathy-deficit/

Holmes, D. L. (2006, December 21). *The Founding Fathers, DeISm, and Christianity | Christianity, Enlightenment & Religion.* Encyclopedia Britannica. https://www.britannica.com/topic/The-Founding-Fathers-Deism-and-Christianity-1272214

Identity Politics (Stanford Encyclopedia of Philosophy). (2020a, July 11). https://plato.stanford.edu/entries/identity-politics/

Identity Politics (Stanford Encyclopedia of Philosophy). (2020b, July 11). https://plato.stanford.edu/entries/identity-politics/

Juntiwasarakij, S. (2018). Framing emerging behaviors influenced by internet celebrity. *Kasetsart Journal of Social Sciences, 39*(3), 550–555. https://doi.org/10.1016/j.kjss.2018.06.014

Kertscher, T. (2020). *Black Lives Matters has become a movement broadly backed by Americans, few of whom would identify as Marxists.* @Politifact. Retrieved March 13, 2024, from https://www.politifact.com/article/2020/jul/21/black-lives-matter-marxist-movement/

Lapin, A. (2024, March 14). What to know about the fiery Jewish reactions to Jonathan Glazer's Oscars speech criticizing Israel. Jewish Telegraphic Agency. https://www.jta.org/2024/03/12/culture/what-to-know-about-the-fiery-jewish-reactions-to-jonathan-glazers-oscars-speech-criticizing-israel

Lavizzo-Mourey, R., Besser, R. E., & Williams, D. R. (2021). Understanding and mitigating health inequities — past, current, and future directions. *The New England Journal of Medicine, 384*(18), 1681–1684. https://doi.org/10.1056/nejmp2008628

Ludden, J. (2023, March 27). Cities may be debating reparations, but here's why most Americans oppose the idea. *NPR.* https://www.npr.org/2023/03/27/1164869576/cities-reparations-white-black-slavery-oppose

MacGillis, A. (2023, December 7). Social media could be contributing to more violence among young people. *ProPublica.* https://www.propublica.org/article/social-media-violence-young-americans

Malik, K. (2020, June 14). "White privilege" is a distraction, leaving racism and power untouched. *The Guardian.* https://www.theguardian.com/commentisfree/2020/jun/14/white-privilege-is-a-lazy-distraction-leaving-racism-and-power-untouched

Mamiya, L. A. (2024, February 17). *Malcolm X | Biography, Nation of Islam, Assassination, & Facts.* Encyclopedia Britannica. https://www.britannica.com/biography/Malcolm-X

Media Violence and Desensitization | Applied Social Psychology (ASP). (2023, March 18). https://sites.psu.edu/aspsy/2023/03/18/media-violence-and-desensitization/

Menczer, F. (2021, October 7). *Here's exactly how social media algorithms can manipulate you.* Big Think. https://bigthink.com/the-present/social-media-algorithms-manipulate-you/

Miller, J. C. (2001). Bowing to Necessities: A History of Manners in America, 1620-1860. By C. Dallett Hemphill (New York and Oxford: Oxford University Press, 1999.x plus 310pp.). *Journal of Social History, 35*(1), 207–208. https://doi.org/10.1353/jsh.2001.0095

Mitchell, T. (2020, June 9). *In U.S., decline of Christianity continues at rapid pace | Pew Research Center.* Pew Research Center's Religion & Public Life Project. https://www.pewresearch.org/religion/2019/10/17/in-u-s-decline-of-christianity-continues-at-rapid-pace/

Mullen, M. (2023, June 27). Jamestown Colony - Facts, founding, Pocahontas | HISTORY. *HISTORY.* https://www.history.com/topics/colonial-america/jamestown

National Institute for Civil Discourse. (2023, May 11). *ABOUT - National Institute for Civil Discourse.* https://nicd.arizona.edu/about/

Normalizing sexual violence through media fuels rape culture – Saratoga Falcon. (2021, November 22). https://saratogafalcon.org/content/normalizing-sexual-violence-through-media-fuels-rape-culture/

Onion, A. (2024, February 27). Civil rights movement Timeline - Timeline & Events | HISTORY. *HISTORY.* https://www.history.com/topics/black-history/civil-rights-movement-timeline

Pailin, D. A., & Manuel, F. E. (2024, February 2). *DEISM | Definition, History, Beliefs, Significance, & Facts.* Encyclopedia Britannica. https://www.britannica.com/topic/Deism

Panreck, H. (2024, March 27). Sunny Hostin accuses Black author arguing for "colorblind America" of being "used as a pawn by the right." Fox News. https://www.foxnews.com/media/sunny-hostin-accuses-black-author-arguing-colorblind-america-being-used-pawn-right

Parks, K. (2024, March 20). New film calling White people "most dangerous animal" on planet bombs at box office. *Fox News.* https://www.foxnews.com/media/new-film-calling-white-people-most-dangerous-animal-planet-bombs-box-office

Peterson, B. (2023, May 19). Rep. Cori Bush says $14 trillion reparations bill will "eliminate the racial wealth gap." *ABC News.* https://abcnews.go.com/Politics/rep-cori-bush-14-trillion-reparations-bill-eliminate/story?id=99390652

Pew Research Center. (2021, March 22). *Majorities in U.S. say Black, Hispanic, Asian people face discrimination | Pew Research Center.* https://www.pewresearch.org/short-reads/2021/03/18/majorities-of-americans-see-at-least-some-discrimination-against-black-hispanic-and-asian-people-in-the-u-s/

Philosiblog, V. a. P. B. (2013, January 15). *Darkness cannot drive out darkness; only light can do that. Hate cannot drive out hate; only love can do that.* Philosiblog. https://philosiblog.com/2013/01/15/darkness-cannot-drive-out-darkness-only-light-can-do-that-hate-cannot-drive-out-hate-only-love-can-do-that/

Philosophy, O., & Philosophy, O. (2023, July 23). Sensationalism: the evil behind the mass media. *Overtime*

Rivara, F. P., Adhia, A., Lyons, V. H., Massey, A., Mills, B., Morgan, E., Simckes, M., & Rowhani-Rahbar, A. (2019). The effects of violence on health. *Health Affairs, 38*(10), 1622–1629. https://doi.org/10.1377/hlthaff.2019.00480

Roy, D. (2022, December 2). Ten graphics that explain the U.S. struggle with migrant flows in 2022. *Council on Foreign Relations.* https://www.cfr.org/article/ten-graphics-explain-us-struggle-migrant-flows-2022

Ruiz, M. (2024, March 28). Jonathan Diller shooting: NYPD sergeants' union tells anti-police Democrats to stay away from funeral. Fox News. https://www.foxnews.com/us/jonathan-diller-shooting-nypd-sergeants-union-tells-anti-police-democrats-stay-away-funeral

Sector, I. (2022, June 30). *How Interfaith Youth Core is building Interfaith America on campus and beyond.* Independent Sector. https://independentsector.org/blog/how-interfaith-youth-core-is-building-interfaith-america-on-campus-and-beyond/#:~:text=Interfaith%20Youth%20Core%20%28IFYC%29%20works%20to%20inspire%2C%20equip%2C,Independent%20Sector%20member%20working%20to%20advance%20interfaith%20cooperation.

Steinbuch, Y. (2020, June 25). Black Lives Matter co-founder describes herself as "trained Marxist." *New York Post.* https://nypost.com/2020/06/25/blm-co-founder-describes-herself-as-trained-marxist/

Stephen. (2023a). *The Rise of Marxism in the 19th Century: An In-Depth Exploration.* Semilla De Botjael. https://19thcentury.us/marxism-in-the-19th-century/

Stephen. (2023b, August 10). The Rise of Marxism in the 19th Century: An In-Depth Exploration - 19th century. *Semilla de Botjael.* https://19thcentury.us/marxism-in-the-19th-century/

Stricklin, C. (2019, August 26). 13 Guiding principles for courageous conversations. *Forbes.* https://www.forbes.com/sites/forbescoachescouncil/2019/08/26/13-guiding-principles-for-courageous-conversations/?sh=657a11174c9f

Sun, Q., Wojcieszak, M., & Davidson, S. (2021). Over-Time trends in incivility on social media: evidence from Political, Non-Political, and Mixed Sub-Reddits over eleven years. *Frontiers in Political Science, 3.* https://doi.org/10.3389/fpos.2021.741605

The Civil Rights Movement | The Post War United States, 1945-1968 | U.S. History Primary Source Timeline | Classroom Materials at the Library of Congress | Library of Congress. (n.d.). The Library of Congress. https://www.loc.gov/classroom-materials/united-states-history-primary-source-timeline/post-war-united-states-1945-1968/civil-rights-movement/

The United States pays reparations every day—just not to Black America. (2022, February 3). Harvard Kennedy School. https://www.hks.harvard.edu/faculty-research/policycast/us-pays-reparations-every-day-just-not-black-america

Thompson, N. (2018, August 25). *Better Angels: the organization out to fight polarization.* Merion West. https://merionwest.com/2018/08/25/better-angels-the-organization-out-to-fight-polarization/

Today, J. T. U. (2023, July 3). "Fairly big problem": Squatters invade homes and refuse to leave. How is this legal? *USA TODAY.* https://www.usatoday.com/story/opinion/2023/07/03/squatters-rights-leave-homeowners-forgotten/70364321007/

Trilling, D. (2022, June 3). *How the media's coverage of political polarization affects voter attitudes.* The Journalist's Resource. https://journalistsresource.org/politics-and-government/medias-coverage-political-polarization-affects-voter-attitudes/

Twenge, J. M. (2023, May 1). How Gen Z changed its views on gender. *TIME.* https://time.com/6275663/generation-z-gender-identity/

Valenzuela, E. (2022, September 19). *Michael Caine saw something special in his Dark Knight trilogy role.* SlashFilm. https://www.slashfilm.com/1005469/michael-caine-saw-something-special-in-his-dark-knight-trilogy-role/

Vanderbilt. (2021, April 7). Civics 101: Keep demagogues out of democracy. *Vanderbilt University.* https://www.vanderbilt.edu/unity/2021/04/07/civics-101-keep-demagogues-out-of-democracy/

Walsh, M. (2020, October 2). *WALSH: President Trump banned critical race theory in federal government. now it needs to be banned in schools.* The Daily Wire. https://www.dailywire.com/news/walsh-president-trump-banned-critical-race-theory-in-federal-government-now-it-needs-to-be-banned-in-schools

Wehner, G. (2024, March 25). Boston activists seeking $15B in reparations, call on "White churches" to commit to extending wealth. *Fox News.* https://www.foxnews.com/politics/boston-activists-seeking-reparations-call-white-churches-commit-extending-wealth

Yahoo is part of the Yahoo family of brands. (2018, June 25). https://news.yahoo.com/apos-apos-not-welcome-anymore-114523010.html?guccounter=1&guce_referrer=aHR0cHM6Ly93d3cuYmluZy5jb20v&guce_referrer_sig=AQAAABoSz9vQQr6Lmlj HJ02C8Q0pVmSFpB0fm3UiO5BBFs3vfoAq83sDLR2Ux8VnFB2 UzdX7sbpin60YPGturejfT2uQDG4y1_nBimGFmz62sewDXnqff nkQhELK4ET-cBICH0mehNwQDKQf5r4zqOaFOPV_l0IQtEkweUTZI9NJWJ0 R